PRAISE FOR
LIFE IN THE BALANCE

This is not a time for Christians to sit and wring their hands. Christians, living up to the highest ideals of their faith, have always defended the weak and vulnerable and eagerly worked to strengthen the vital institutions of civil society. Joni Eareckson Tada and her team work tirelessly for the equal protection of every innocent human being at every stage of development and in every condition. In *Life in the Balance*, they equip the Church to think biblically about these issues. It's where the rubber meets the road. It is where the battle really is joined.

Chuck Colson
Founder of Prison Fellowship and The Chuck Colson Center for Christian Worldview

In *Life in the Balance*, Joni and Friends provide an unflinching look at complex cultural and global issues surrounding the sanctity of life and how we as God's people can think about these hot topics. Stories of oppression, abuse, depression, neglect and disability showcase the way God redeems even the darkest hours to inform, change and grow us when we submit to His eternal perspective. I have seen firsthand how the themes of this book have been lived out in Joni's courageous leadership through Joni and Friends, at Biola University, and throughout the world.

Barry Corey
President, Biola University, La Mirada, CA

When Joni speaks, I listen. What Joni writes, I read. When she commends the insights of like-minded friends, I pay attention. And so should you. Unable to run here and there with perfectly formed limbs, Joni has spent countless hours contemplating *Life in the Balance*. As her life has grown richer and deeper, she has been empowered to bless multitudes out of the overflow of a life spent in the presence of the Master.

Hank Hanegraaff
President of the Christian Research Institute
Host of the *Bible Answer Man* Broadcast

Life in the Balance poses a crucial question: What do you say when faced with one of life's "sticky dilemmas"—those hot button, complex social issues of our day? How do you respond when those difficult questions enter your own life? Abortion, autism, the stem cell debate . . . these issues and more are examined through the lens of Scripture, practical application, and reasoned scientific information. And who better to lead this timely discussion than my good friend Joni Eareckson Tada? Decades in a wheelchair have given her wisdom, knowledge, insight and compassion for such a time as this. Joni and her friends have done the Christian community a valuable service in compiling this heart-and-soul-challenging book.

Max Lucado
Pastor and Bestselling Author of *Outlive Your Life*

If you are anything like me—and in this case I suspect you are—reading a comprehensive book on bioethics is not on your "bucket list" of things to do in life. Most of us can barely begin to grasp all of the biblical, philosophical, moral, scientific and emotionally personal issues related to the ethics of birth, life and death. Yet humanity cannot afford for the followers of Jesus Christ to sit on the sidelines while scientific developments and "survival of the fittest" values race forward!

As a pastor, I have struggled to get my own head and heart around these sensitive issues—let alone to help others grapple with them. *Life in the Balance* ended that for me! This captivating book tackles the toughest issues related to bioethics and disability. Joni and her team all bring tremendous credibility to the areas about which they each write. They are not merely theorists but also individuals who have faced these issues personally. They graciously weave heart-wrenching personal stories, scientific information, biblical truths and practical applications into an easily understood resource for all. Ultimately, each reader will be challeng[ed] from conception to death, as fearfully and wonderfully made by God Himself!

Shawn Thornton
Senior Pastor, Calvary Community Church, Westlake Village, CA
www.calvarycc.org

PAT VERBAL, GENERAL EDITOR

Joni Eareckson Tada
& FRIENDS

Biblical Answers for the Issues of Our Day

LIFE IN THE
BALANCE
LEADER'S GUIDE

RAISE AWARENESS & MOVE PEOPLE TO ACTION

Regal

From Gospel Light
Ventura, California, U.S.A.

Published by Regal
From Gospel Light
Ventura, California, U.S.A.
www.regalbooks.com
Printed in the U.S.A.

Written by Pat Verbal with contributions from Chonda Ralston, Sheila Harper, Rebecca Olson

Rights for publishing this book outside the U.S.A. or in non-English languages are administered by Gospel Light Worldwide,
an international not-for-profit ministry. For additional information, please visit www.glww.org,
email info@glww.org, or write to Gospel Light Worldwide, 1957 Eastman Avenue, Ventura, CA 93003, U.S.A.

To order copies of this book and other Regal products in bulk quantities, please contact us at 1-800-446-7735.

LIFE in the Balance . . .

Everything that goes into a LIFE of pleasing God

has already been miraculously given to us

by getting to know . . . the One who invites us to God. . . .

We were also given absolutely terrific promises—

your tickets to participation in the LIFE of God. . . .

So don't lose a minute of building on what you've been given,

complementing your basic faith with good character,

spiritual understanding, alert discipline,

passionate patience, reverent wonder,

warm friendliness, and generous love. . . .

Without these qualities you can't see what's right before you. . . .

So, friends, confirm God's invitation to you, his choice of you.

Don't put it off; do it now.

Do this, and you'll have your LIFE on a firm footing . . .

into the eternal kingdom of our Master and Savior, Jesus Christ.

2 Peter 1:5-11, *The Message*

CONTENTS

A NOTE FROM JONI

Never before in history have we been so bombarded with such sticky ethical dilemmas. Today's moral problems aren't discussed in dry abstract theory; they are often haggled out in emotional counseling sessions or parking-lot arguments after work. They surface when a teenager suffers a life-altering accident, when an out-of-work father decides to leave a suicide note, or when the parents of a child with a disability can't find a church willing to include their family. Life's tough issues often catch us off guard—like when we're just having coffee with a friend or standing in a line at the store. We overhear a cell-phone conversation and realize once again how much people need help. We all need wisdom and guidance.

During my years at Joni and Friends, I've met amazing people—most of them, like me, have looked hard into the Bible for guidance after a tragic accident, debilitating illness or other painful crisis. Spending time with them has inspired me. Watching the way they've handled the tough issues in their lives has driven me even deeper into the Word of God. So in 2007 when God led us to produce our first Joni and Friends TV series, I knew I wanted to highlight their stories. We later realized that their examples would serve as perfect illustration for the tough questions in a study like *Life in the Balance*.

And, oh, has God used the stories of these people to help others gain a biblical worldview on everything from abortion to autism . . . from euthanasia to eugenics . . . from victims of violence to young people absorbed with self.

Thank you for taking up the challenges in *Life in the Balance*. We stand with you in prayer as you help participants bring God back into the public marketplace by addressing some of the hottest topics of our day.

GETTING STARTED

Whether you live in a rural area or a booming urban metropolis, you'll agree that the world is full of lonely people. Jesus felt compassion for the masses following Him and said, "they were like sheep without a shepherd" (Mark 6:34). Are we indeed like sheep?

By some accounts, we're the most educated, most informed, most engaged generation that ever lived on planet Earth. With advances in computer technologies, school textbooks will soon be a thing of the past. Churches build huge edifices and hire production directors to manage multiple services for thousands of worshipers. There is a bank on nearly every street corner and even small-town malls are crowded with determined shoppers. So with all this activity going on, how can it be said that we're like stumbling sheep, which so easily lose their way?

In all our preparation for the "good life," we work very hard at avoiding the rocky places. We believe that if we run hard enough in the right direction, we'll reach the "best" life has to offer. Sadly, it's just not true! Sometimes we run into brick walls of our own making. Other times we're led into darkness by those who would do us harm for their own pleasure or profit. Yes, we surely need a Shepherd who speaks the truth. God's Word is the source of truth, offering answers to today's questions for personal growth, healthy relationships and life's purpose.

Our daily news includes stories of people who face physical, mental and emotional crises resulting in life-long suffering. Many of these dilemmas are compounded by medical technology, ethical conflicts and social injustices. In *Life in the Balance,* group members will meet people who have faced life's toughest battles and emerged victorious. In their testimonies, the participants will begin to understand God's designs for our sufferings as they apply to each one of us, as well as to the family of God. They'll gain new confidence to speak out on critical issues that are presented in opposition to the Word of God. They'll also discover that one person *can* make a difference.

> *Life is an exciting business, and it is most exciting when it is lived for others.*
> HELEN KELLER

Becoming a Life-Coach Leader

If you've ever watched a tightrope walker at the circus, you know the importance of maintaining a delicate balance at tricky heights. The performer must continuously adjust the bend of the poll to keep moving toward the safety of the platform. Keep that image in mind

People Need the Lord . . .

- A fear of being dehumanized haunts the 660 million people living with disabilities in the world.[1]
- There are 120,000 babies born each year with birth defects.[2]
- One in 150 children is born with autism.[3]
- Over 33,000 U.S. military personnel have been wounded in action since 2001.[4]
- Girls and women are exploited, abused, and sold into slavery and prostitution.
- Auto accidents, industrial injuries and crimes thrust people into the darkness of depression and fear.

as you prepare to introduce the eight probing topics in this course: violence, autism, self-image, the stem cell debate, abortion, eugenics and genocide, end-of-life issues, and materialism. You may be thinking, *Can't we just stick to topics like grace, love, joy and peace?* We could—if that summed up our lives. But there are good reasons why Christians must engage in the touch issues of our day, such as . . .

- The enormous power and pervasion of the liberal media
- The numerous conflicting opinions between science and religion
- The morality of emerging technologies
- The diverse and secular nature of modern education

And even more importantly, Jesus set an example for us to follow. He was engaged in the lives of hurting people. Of the 35 recorded miracles of Jesus in the New Testament, 23 of them involved people with disabilities such as mental illness, blindness, deafness, paralysis, a withered hand and leprosy. These give us a clue to the heart of God and the priority He places on suffering. A true New Testament church will sincerely value all people, reaching out to relieve pain and injustice as Jesus did.

Participants will not enter your group as blank slates. They will have ideas and opinions that can be as varied as the issues themselves. Don't let that discourage you, but welcome the opportunity to explore each topic in light of the Word of God. As you prayerfully prepare for each session, ask God to give you fresh insight. Part of your job is to teach participants to think for themselves and to ask harder questions of news reports that they may have taken for granted before this study.

How to Read the News

Teachers often tell students that the first thing they have to learn at school is to learn how to study. While that's great advice, Christians can ask for help. It's called discernment, and we can ask God, as Solomon did, to give each of us "a discerning heart" (1 Kings 3:9). Discernment is the act of being able to grasp and comprehend something that is obscure. Encourage participants to ask for discernment as they grow in critical thinking skills, especially as they consider news reports in the paper, on television or on the internet. The following questions will be helpful:

- What is my purpose for reading this article? Why was I drawn to it?
- Is the writer a credible source on this topic? What is his or her purpose?
- Do the ideas or concepts connect and reach a logical conclusion?
- Is the information supported by credible sources that I can respect?
- What is the nature of man, God and truth in the piece?
- Are the facts in line with absolute truths that I believe?
- What does God want me to think (or do) regarding what I've read?

Share these questions with the group you lead so the participants will be more sensitive to the news.

Counseling Tips and Follow-Up

As a leader you must have a strong and vibrant relationship with Jesus Christ and an unwavering commitment to evangelize and disciple people from all walks of life. Your integrity and desire to display the fruit of God's Spirit in your own life will set the tone for your group.

It's only natural that when we discuss topics that touch people's lives, some people will express emotional pain. Dr. Mark W. Baker, Executive Director of the La Vie Counseling Center, says this about the problem of pain:

Even though God created emotions to help us connect to Him and to others, it doesn't always work that way. Sometimes when the pain of suffering is too great, the very emotions that were intended to bond us to others actually create a separation between us. This is not due to a lack of faith; it is due to an emotional reaction to intense pain. It is important to understand that the feeling of isolation is a psychological property of trauma.[5]

Expressions of emotional pain, then, are natural and not necessarily expressions of loss of faith.

13

In his book *Jesus, the Greatest Therapist Who Ever Lived,* Dr. Baker suggests ways to help people do the "grief work," which must be done to learn to trust God and live in His peace. If you're hesitant to lead discussions that may become emotional, reading this book will be a tremendous help. However, as group leader, you are not expected to have all of the answers—no one does. Your role is to model the compassion of Jesus Christ so that others will find a safe place to be themselves. In each session of this leader's guide, you'll find helpful advice to do this as it relates to the topics.

It is a good idea to speak with your pastor and/or discipleship leaders before you begin this study. Ask for their prayer support and advice if it should become obvious that a member of your group needs additional counseling. A first step might be asking him or her to meet with you and another trusted friend for coffee or a soft drink. Reaching out in Christian friendship is always appropriate. Second, encourage the person to meet with one of the pastors who takes counseling appointments.

Every church should maintain a list of recommended Christian counselors and family therapists in the community. Due to liability issues, it is wise to encourage an individual to choose for himself or herself from the list.

What If a Participant Doesn't Agree with the Content?

It is almost inevitable that at least one participant will not agree with something that is presented in one of the sessions. A wise man once said that if two people in a couple agree, then one of them is not necessary. Our goal in writing *Life in the Balance* was not to seek perfect unity but to encourage people to think about biblical truth in light of today's ethical dilemmas.

You may want to post and refer to these verses from 2 Timothy in class each week:

Keep reminding them of these things. Warn them before God against quarreling about words; it is of no value, and only ruins those who listen. Do your best to present yourself to God as one approved, a workman who does not need to be ashamed and who correctly handles the word of truth. Avoid godless chatter, because those who indulge in it will become more and more ungodly (vv. 14-16).

Be ready to exercise your role as leader and suggest that more study, as well as private discussions, may be required. The writers of these materials have had many discussions on these issues . . . and, yes, some debates, too! You can trust that the content reflects wisdom and experience that will benefit your group.

What If a Participant Dominates the Discussion?

Occasionally, you may find that one person in your group appears to talk so much that no other group member has a chance to say anything. Approach each situation with the attitude that such a domineering person means well. Be respectful. Allow him or her enough time to make a point, but do not give up control of the group that *you* have committed to lead. Watch the person's body language and listen for any hidden messages. If it's appropriate, ask for others to comment on the point being expressed. In the end, you must politely explain that every person should have the opportunity to share his or her ideas during the discussion and then move on. If the person continues to try to control the discussion, try calling the person during the week just to talk. The extra attention is often what is needed, and it can make a big difference for the whole group.

Prayer Guidelines

As the familiar hymn says, "What a friend we have in Jesus, all our sin and grief to bear! What a privilege to carry everything to God in prayer!" There will be times during this study when the stories and statistics are so painful that a cloud of hopelessness descends on your group. This is not a time to end the session in despair. It's an opportunity to call on God for divine intervention, praying specifically for people groups or an individual's need. Regardless of what a person can do to relieve another's heartache, nothing is as powerful as prayer. As you begin your group prayer time, you may want to read the prayers at the end of each chapter in *Life in the Balance*. In lieu of or in addition to this prayer, you could assign a prayer coordinator to keep a list of prayer requests and answers to prayer throughout the study and to update the list in group emails. (To protect each person's privacy, be careful to limit the information that is included in such emails.) God knows each of us intimately and has power to work all things for our good (see Rom. 8:28).

Course Overview

SESSION	TOPIC	FEATURING	KEY VERSES
1. Life's Sticky Dilemma	Introduction	Joni Eareckson Tada	Proverbs 2:1-5
2. When Life Isn't Fair	Violence in the Streets	Vicky Olivas	Luke 23:34
3. Making Sense of Autism	Autism	Families affected by autism	Matthew 19:14

SESSION	TOPIC	FEATURING	KEY VERSES
4. Self-Image in a Fickle Culture	Self-Image	Holly Strother	Ephesians 2:10
5. Searching for the Greater Good	The Stem Cell Debate	Laura Dominguez	Psalm 25:4-5
6. The Truth Behind the Pain of Abortion	Abortion	David and Nancy Guthrie	Psalm 139:13-14
7. A Calloused Conscience	Eugenics and Genocide	Robin Hiser	Proverbs 31:8
8. From Obscurity to Celebrity by Way of Tragedy	End-of-Life Issues	Terri Schiavo	Proverbs 12:28
9. I've Got Questions About the American Dream	Materialism	Nick Vujicic	Matthew 6:31-33
10. Now What?	Advocacy	Joni Eareckson Tada	Micah 6:8

Session Format and Options

The format of this study is one 2-hour session per week for 10 consecutive weeks, including 30-minute readings of *Life in the Balance* at home and 1½ hours in small-group sessions. It would be ideal if your group has time to do 12 weeks, since two of the DVD segments are done in two parts of 30 minutes each. If you must choose to do fewer sessions, ask participants for their input in choosing the topics they are most interested in studying. Whatever number of sessions you decide, sessions 1 and 10 should be used with the DVD segments to introduce all of the topics and to conclude with a call to Christian service. Each session consists of the following sections:

1. **Opening:** Each session begins with an opening prayer and an activity that leads into that week's viewing of the *Life in the Balance* DVD.

2. **Life in the Word:** In this section, group members will begin to examine the issue being presented in the DVD in light of God's Word.

3. **Achieving Personal Balance:** Members will now begin to build on what they have learned in the previous section and consider what place the issue has in their lives as followers of Christ.

4. **Balancing Faith and Culture:** The members will conclude the session by examining the issue on a more personal level and begin to consider it in terms of how it affects their day-to-day lives.

As you get to know the group, you can vary the schedule. However, please build in time for fellowship before or after session times. The session outlines are designed to get participants talking about the topics before watching the DVDs. The DVD segments for sessions 1 and 10 are both 15 minutes, but the other eight are 25 minutes each. However, don't cut any session short, because if you do, the entire group will miss out on participating in the lively discussion that each of these topics is sure to provoke.

Welcome and Opening Prayer	Opening	5 minutes
Opening Activity	Introduction	10 minutes
Life in the Balance DVD	Viewing	25 minutes
Life in the Word	Bible Study	15 minutes
Achieving Personal Balance	Discussion	15 minutes
Balancing Faith and Culture	Application	15 minutes
Closing Prayer	Closing	5 minutes
	Total Session	**90 minutes**

This schedule is ideal for daytime or evening sessions, even for couples who need time to drop off or pick up children in child care. (Due to the nature of the discussions during each session, it is recommended that young children do not attend.)

At the end of each chapter is an "Evaluating the Session" section for you to use to determine how your time with the group went and whether or not the session objectives were met. Use this evaluation to analyze which areas could be improved during the group time to help you better communicate the topics being presented. (Helpful resources and websites are also included for your reference.)

How to Use the *Life in the Balance* DVD

The DVD that came with this leader's guide contains the videos for all 10 sessions, as well as some extra features listed in the menu. As you review the videos, you'll notice that while some videos closely follow the discussion outlined in the chapters, others complement the topic under discussion. This provides options for you to emphasize the parts that work best with your group. In the same way, some of the discussion questions draw attention to the issues in the chapters, while others consider the people in the stories.

If a member of your group would like to use one of the DVD segments to minister to a friend or family member, please let your group know that individual DVDs are available for purchase at the Joni and Friends website (see www.joniandfriendstv.org). Your group may consider purchasing a set for your church library or a local rehab center as a service project. It is one more way your church can share the gospel of Jesus Christ with your community.

THE MANHATTAN DECLARATION[1]

A Summary

Preamble

Christians are heirs of a 2,000-year tradition of proclaiming God's word, seeking justice in our societies, resisting tyranny, and reaching out with compassion to the poor, oppressed and suffering.

While fully acknowledging the imperfections and shortcomings of Christian institutions and communities in all ages, we claim the heritage of those Christians who defended innocent life by rescuing discarded babies from trash heaps in Roman cities and publicly denouncing the Empire's sanctioning of infanticide. We remember with reverence those believers who sacrificed their lives by remaining in Roman cities to tend the sick and dying during the plagues, and who died bravely in the coliseums rather than deny their Lord.

After the barbarian tribes overran Europe, Christian monasteries preserved not only the Bible but also the literature and art of Western culture. It was Christians who combated the evil of slavery: Papal edicts in the 16th and 17th centuries decried the practice of slavery and first excommunicated anyone involved in the slave trade; evangelical Christians in England, led by John Wesley and William Wilberforce, put an end to the slave trade in that country. Christians under Wilberforce's leadership also formed hundreds of societies for helping the poor, the imprisoned, and child laborers chained to machines.

In Europe, Christians challenged the divine claims of kings and successfully fought to establish the rule of law and balance of governmental powers, which made modern democracy possible. And in America, Christian women stood at the vanguard of the suffrage movement. The great civil rights crusades of the 1950s and 60s were led by Christians claiming the Scriptures and asserting the glory of the image of God in every human being regardless of race, religion, age or class.

This same devotion to human dignity has led Christians in recent decades to work to end the dehumanizing scourge of human trafficking and sexual slavery, bring compassionate care to AIDS sufferers in Africa, and assist in a myriad of other human rights causes—from providing clean water in developing nations to providing homes for tens of thousands of children orphaned by war, disease and gender discrimination.

Like those who have gone before us in the faith, Christians today are called to proclaim the Gospel of costly grace, to protect the intrinsic dignity of the human person and to stand

19

for the common good. In being true to its own calling, the call to discipleship, the church through service to others can make a profound contribution to the public good.

The Declaration

Christians, when they have lived up to the highest ideals of their faith, have defended the weak and vulnerable and worked tirelessly to protect and strengthen vital institutions of civil society, beginning with the family.

We are Orthodox, Catholic, and evangelical Christians who have united at this hour to reaffirm fundamental truths about justice and the common good, and to call upon our fellow citizens, believers and non-believers alike, to join us in defending them. These truths are (1) the sanctity of human life, (2) the dignity of marriage as the conjugal union of husband and wife, and (3) the rights of conscience and religious liberty. Inasmuch as these truths are foundational to human dignity and the wellbeing of society, they are inviolable and non-negotiable. Because they are increasingly under assault from powerful forces in our culture, we are compelled today to speak out forcefully in their defense, and to commit ourselves to honoring them fully no matter what pressures are brought upon us and our institutions to abandon or compromise them. We make this commitment not as partisans of any political group but as followers of Jesus Christ, the crucified and risen Lord, who is the Way, the Truth, and the Life.

Human Life

The lives of the unborn, the disabled, and the elderly are ever more threatened. While public opinion has moved in a pro-life direction, powerful and determined forces are working to expand abortion, embryo-destructive research, assisted suicide, and euthanasia. Although the protection of the weak and vulnerable is the first obligation of government, the power of government is today often enlisted in the cause of promoting what Pope John Paul II called "the culture of death." We pledge to work unceasingly for the equal protection of every innocent human being at every stage of development and in every condition. We will refuse to permit ourselves or our institutions to be implicated in the taking of human life and we will support in every possible way those who, in conscience, take the same stand.

Marriage

The institution of marriage, already wounded by promiscuity, infidelity and divorce, is at risk of being redefined and thus subverted. Marriage is the original and most important institution for sustaining the health, education, and welfare of all. Where marriage erodes, social pathologies rise. The impulse to redefine marriage is a symptom, rather than the cause, of the erosion of the marriage culture. It reflects a loss of understanding of the meaning of marriage as embodied in our civil law as well as our religious traditions. Yet it is critical that the impulse be resisted, for yielding to it would mean abandoning the possibility of restoring a sound understanding of marriage and, with it, the hope of rebuilding a healthy marriage culture. It would lock into place the false and destructive belief that marriage is all about romance and other adult satisfactions, and more [than] not, in any intrinsic way, about the unique character and value of acts and relationships whose meaning is shaped by their aptness for the generation, promotion and protection of life. Marriage is not a "social construction," but is rather an objective reality—the covenantal union of husband and wife—that it is the duty of the law to recognize, honor, and protect.

Religious Liberty

Freedom of religion and the rights of conscience are gravely jeopardized. The threat to these fundamental principles of justice is evident in efforts to weaken or eliminate conscience protections for healthcare institutions and professionals, and in antidiscrimination statutes that are used as weapons to force religious institutions, charities, businesses, and service providers either to accept (and even facilitate) activities and relationships they judge to be immoral, or go out of business. Attacks on religious liberty are dire threats not only to individuals, but also to the institutions of civil society including families, charities, and religious communities. The health and wellbeing of such institutions provide an indispensable buffer against the overweening power of government and is essential to the flourishing of every other institution—including government itself—on which society depends.

Unjust Laws

As Christians, we believe in law and we respect the authority of earthly rulers. We count it as a special privilege to live in a democratic society where the moral claims of the law on us are even stronger in virtue of the rights of all citizens to participate in the political process. Yet even in a democratic regime, laws can be unjust. And from the beginning, our faith has taught that civil disobedience is required in the face of gravely unjust laws or laws that purport to require us to do what is unjust or otherwise immoral. Such laws lack the power to bind in conscience because they can claim no authority beyond that of sheer human will.

Therefore, let it be known that we will not comply with any edict that compels us or the institutions we lead to participate in or facilitate abortions, embryo-destructive research, assisted suicide, euthanasia, or any other act that violates the principle of the profound, inherent, and equal dignity of every member of the human family.

Further, let it be known that we will not bend to any rule forcing us to bless immoral sexual partnerships, treat them as marriages or the equivalent, or refrain from proclaiming the truth, as we know it, about morality, marriage, and the family.

Further, let it be known that we will not be intimidated into silence or acquiescence or the violation of our consciences by any power on earth, be it cultural or political regardless of the consequences to ourselves. We will fully and ungrudgingly render to Caesar what is Caesar's. But under no circumstances will we render to Caesar what is God's.

Drafting Committee

Robert George, Professor, McCormick Professor of Jurisprudence, Princeton University
Timothy George, Professor, Beeson Divinity School, Samford University
Chuck Colson, Founder, the Chuck Colson Center for Christian Worldview (Lansdowne, VA)

RAISE AWARENESS & MOVE PEOPLE TO ACTION

LIFE IN THE BALANCE

LEADER'S GUIDE

LIFE'S STICKY DILEMMAS: INTRODUCTION

If you call out for insight and cry aloud for understanding . . . and search for it as for hidden treasure,
then you will understand the fear of the Lord and the knowledge of God.

PROVERBS 2:1-5

Life-Coach Leaders

In the first chapter of *Life in the Balance*, Joni Eareckson Tada uses her own story to ease readers into discussions on cultural issues that are dear to her heart. Although few participants will directly relate to being confined to a wheelchair, your group will respond to the general topics, because they will strike a chord with each person. Whether we want to admit it or not, we all have to deal with these issues, for our lives are interconnected. The "It's my life!" crowd forgets that what happens to them *does* ultimately impact the rest of us. It's a constant theme running through the traumatic yet amazing stories your group will hear throughout this course.

This interdependence is beautifully illustrated in the joy and sorrow of Nick, who was born with no arms and no legs, or of Vicky, whose life was turned upside down after being shot during a job interview. You'll help participants get to know a 16-year-old girl who almost died in a car accident, and some brave parents who are successfully raising children with autism spectrum disorders. Help your group to see that, in every case, these individuals learned to depend on faithful Christians whom God placed in their lives, but more importantly, they came to trust God as their source of strength and truth. Joni calls these folks God's object lessons. She says, "Ministry is messy. God plops people with disabilities in the midst of a congregation—a hand grenade that blows apart the picture-perfectness of the church. But these disenfranchised folks are the 'indispensable' part of the body."

"Disenfranchised" describes those who are deprived of some legal right or a privilege. This deprivation can happen as we attempt to distance ourselves from hurting people, but Joni says that God's plan is just the opposite. Those who struggle with pain and loneliness, with injustice and hopelessness, are indispensable to our personal growth in grace and character. However, many times the Church feels paralyzed to do anything or too uninformed to speak out. You will help your group (and your church) begin to understand what the Bible says about embracing hurting people and helping change one life at a time.

What Are the Session Objectives?

In this opening introductory session, participants will . . .

- Consider the tough questions that come up in everyday conversations
- Define an ethical, or moral, dilemma
- See the connection between human rights and social justice
- Pray for a greater capacity to love and serve people

Why Should Participants Care?

The news is full of sticky dilemmas. Some people are so enthralled by each juicy detail that they become news junkies. Other people are so turned off by what they view as negative and salacious reporting that they want no part of the news. One's background and personality play a huge role in these choices, and a lot of participants in your group will fall in the middle of these two extremes. Regardless of how they relate to the news, most people would say they don't have time in their busy schedules to do anything about the issues anyway.

However, as the participants slow down and truly think as they read, they will discover that at the very core of the hottest topics of our day is an attack on our Judeo-Christian faith. Urge your group to exercise mental muscle as they study today's ethical dilemmas. It's time for all Christians to truly understand what it means to take up their cross and follow Jesus (see Luke 9:23).

Life in Real Time: How to Read the News

Help participants understand a bit about the general history of written communication: From symbols drawn on cave walls 30,000 years ago to the first alphabet created by the Egyptians in 2,000 B.C., man has always found ways to spread the latest news. The first newspapers (or newsletters) were printed in the 1600s and publication of items worthy of note spread from Europe to the American colonies. News was sticky business even back then, greatly influencing public opinion and ultimately contributing to the Revolutionary War.

Fast forward to the twenty-first century, and news topics continue to incite controversy. America's founding fathers sought to create a nation that would protect our human rights and define our religious freedoms. Many gave their lives to uphold these values, which are once again being threatened. These dangers were recently described in a new document, The Manhattan Declaration, published in 2009. (See a summary of the declaration at the beginning of this leader's guide.) Its writers sought to articulate a clear biblical position, which has become a line drawn in the sand for thousands of believers in three areas: life, traditional marriage and religious liberty.

There is nothing magical about this declaration, yet it has become a unifying voice for more than 400,000 Christians who have signed it. Not everyone will recognize the need for such a document to express their convictions, and they too should be respected. While there are several references to this important document throughout this study, it is not vital to teaching the sessions. It is, however, as with all of the material, designed to better equip you as the leader and should be used at your discretion.

Leader Checklist

- ❑ Name tags and pens
- ❑ Bibles
- ❑ The front page of several newspapers
- ❑ Copies of session 1 discussion questions
- ❑ DVD keyed to session 1, "Life's Sticky Dilemma"

OVERVIEW

Welcome and Opening Prayer

As participants enter this first session, ask them to wear nametags. If everyone is new, take time for introductions. Thank them for coming and open in prayer, asking God to open their hearts and minds for understanding and that they will begin to look in a new way at the tough issues that will be presented.

Opening Activity

Pass out the front page of several newspapers, and ask volunteers to read headlines that they think illustrate how our lives can get out of balance. Briefly call attention to the sin and suffering that are often described in these stories. At the core of most disturbing headlines of our day, we find man placing "self" on the throne that is reserved for the Lord of the universe. When this occurs there is no such thing as absolute truth—everyone is logically free to do whatever seems right in his or her own eyes. Humankind's personal rights become the end-all, be-all. We insist on our right to be respected . . . to be understood . . . to have life go our way.

Introduction to "Life's Sticky Dilemma" on the *Life in the Balance* DVD

Give each member a copy of the session 1 discussion questions (see pages 37-38), and then ask the group the first discussion question.

Discussion Question #1

Where do you turn to get the news? How do you interpret what you read or watch?

Answers may include newspapers, magazines, television news programs and/or Internet coverage. The responses will vary, but the question will give you a good idea of how informed group members are on current events. (See "How to Read the News" in the previous section.) Read aloud Proverbs 2:1-5, and then show the session 1 segment on the *Life in the Balance* DVD.

In the session 1 video, Joni relates to participants by welcoming them into her office where she checks her emails and keeps up with news. Viewers will get a rare glimpse at messages she's received from some of the friends you'll meet throughout the study.

Joni also reveals her own vulnerability as she talks about being told she would never walk again or use her hands, and how her depression turned into despair. She reached a place where she didn't want to live in a wheelchair, paralyzed for the rest of her life. She wanted to die! Joni admits that she even begged her high school friends to help her end her life because she couldn't live in such misery.

Thankfully, God placed around Joni people who weren't afraid of her questions. They helped her get to the bottom of her despair and discouragement. Participants will be encouraged to do the same for others who have suffered as a result of violence, disability or injustice. Joni will encourage you to make prayer a key focus of this study. These topics strike close to home for many of us and should bring us to our knees with hearts of compassion toward one another.

Let the group know that as a well-known disability advocate, Joni often takes part in news broadcasts (such as her appearance on the *Larry King Live* show in 2009) to discuss the stem cell debate. Some programs with Joni can be viewed on YouTube. Now ask the group discussion question #2.

Discussion Question #2
Has anyone ever asked you what you believe about one of these issues?

Violence

Autism

Self-Image

Stem Cell Research

Abortion

Genocide

Life Worth

Materialism

On the discussion question sheet, ask the participants to rate these topics using the following scale:

1.   I don't think much about it.
2.   It is somewhat important to me.
3.   I know people who are coping with it.
4.   It keeps me awake at night.

Ask a few volunteers to share their experiences before continuing on to the next section.

Life in the Word

Begin this section by asking the following discussion question with the group.

Discussion Question #3
*Do you believe that God's Word provides truth and answers
to all these questions?*

Allow time for the members to respond. Ask a person in the group to read Psalm 119:105 and Romans 10:17, and then allow time for participants to express any feelings of despair over the serious issues that will be covered in this study, understanding that at times these issues can seem overwhelming and make one feel hopeless.

Continue by stating that the people the members will meet in this study would answer a resounding *yes* to this question. But they didn't always feel that way! They had doubts that nearly swallowed them up in oceans of despair—waves of anger and SOS calls to God, when there was nowhere else to turn. They know what it means to join the Hall of Faith described in Hebrews 11, but at the same time, they understand that they have not yet arrived.

It takes great faith to believe in a great God! Someone described faith this way:

FORSAKING
ALL
I
TAKE
HIM

Hebrews 11 ends by saying that all the "heroes" listed continued to live by faith in spite of the fact that they had not received what had been promised. Their stories remind each of us that faith is not a destination, but a journey.

Achieving Personal Balance

Transition into this next section by asking the members discussion question #4.

Discussion Question #4

Even the lives of followers of Christ can get out of balance at times.
How do you handle this when it happens?

Explain to the group that we've all been there at one time or another. Life seems to be going great when all of a sudden the unexpected happens, and we're dazed. It can be as simple as a reassignment at work or a child with the chicken pox, and our orderly plans are thrown off-kilter. Our morning quiet time that had been so sweet faded under the pressures of the day. Point out to the group that these things may seem small in light of the troubles that they'll learn about in this study, but God cares about the tiniest sparrow, and He cares for each of them.

Discussion Question #5

Steve told Joni, "God permits what He hates to accomplish what He loves."
Have you ever witnessed a time when this happened to someone?

Have someone in the group read aloud 1 Peter 2:21. God permitted what He hated (a cruel cross) to accomplish what He prized (glorifying His mercy and winning our salvation). Joni says, "God permitted what He despised—my wheelchair—to accomplish something that He loved—my character honed, my faith refined and my hope in Christ cemented." Ask participants to complete this sentence: "In my life God permits _____ to accomplish _____." Conclude by reading Psalm 37:4 and discussing how this can be true in tough situations.

Balancing Faith and Culture

Begin this final section in this week's study by having the group discuss the following questions.

Discussion Question #6

How would you define an ethical dilemma?

Allow one or two volunteers to respond, and then explain to your group that an ethical, or moral, dilemma is a question of moral choice—right or wrong, good or evil, justice or virtue—

and how one arrives at this decision. For example, in the stem cell debate there are ethical questions about whether fertilized embryos have the same rights as any human being, or can they be disposed of with no moral consequence. Another ethical battle is played out in living color in motion pictures, in television programs and on Internet websites where "wrong" is often sold as "the best thing going." As a result, the moral generation gap continues to grow.

As Christians we look to God's Word for moral truths to guide our choices and actions. When we see prejudice in our world, we speak out on behalf of those who were created in the image of God. When a friend threatens suicide, we tell them God's moral absolute, "Thou shall not kill." As we are faced with voting-ballot choices that seek to redefine traditional marriage, we look to God's plan for the family and vote our Christian conscience. Read 1 Peter 3:15, and briefly discuss how this passage applies to ethical dilemmas.

Discussion Question #7
How are our culture's ethical debates putting the health of our communities and families at risk?

Have participants look again at the foreword of *Life in the Balance,* where Chuck Colson writes:

One of the great dangers in our society today is that we are minimizing the importance of human life. Of course, we all know the debate about abortion—this debate has been front and center for 30 years, as well it should be. But the assault on human life spreads way beyond the abortion issue. The moment we begin to say that we want to do the greatest good for the greatest number of people; the moment we want utilitarian ethics to guide our decisions, then people get marginalized. People on the fringes of our society get lost and forgotten.

Ask participants if they can think of a person who has been marginalized by society. Remind them that these people are not "out there somewhere" but are a part of every community. During the course of this study, they're going to get a firsthand glimpse into the lives of the weak and meet those who many would say have a life that is not worth living.

Discussion Question #8
How can the Church be a force for change when our society is at stake?

Encourage participants to share ways their church is making a difference in the lives of people who are disenfranchised. One way their church might be taking this step in the right direction is by offering this study. Maybe the pastor recommended it because he or she counsels families caught in crises and believes that more can be done to ease their suffering.

Tell the group that when a church asks Joni and Friends for help to start a disability ministry, a parent support group or a special-needs program for kids, the organization encourages the church to conduct a survey of its members to assess the church's needs. A survey can identify needs in the congregation, as well as those people who can be reached with the gospel of Jesus Christ. God's family has always had more to offer because ultimately Jesus is the only way to healing and hope.

> *We are not to simply bandage the wounds of victims beneath the wheels of injustice, but we are to drive a spoke into the wheel itself.*
> DIETRICH BONHOEFFER

Closing Prayer

Conclude the session by praying that God will use this study to show you His truths regarding these difficult issues. Pray that each participant might be a "good ambassador for [Christ] in a high-tech society" (Jas. 1:5). Ask God to "equip [us] with everything good for doing his will, and may he work in us what is pleasing to him, through Jesus Christ, to whom be glory forever and ever" (Heb. 13:21).

After the prayer, share with the group the fact that this study will prove to be anything but boring, and that next week the topic will be violence in the streets. Encourage participants to read chapter 2 of *Life in the Balance* for your next session. Recruit a prayer coordinator to begin a prayer list for the group, and invite participants to share email prayer requests as they arise in the coming week.

Evaluating the Session

When the following objectives for this study have been met, participants will be able to set biblical standards for living that are pleasing to God. This is not easy to accomplish, but if it were easy, it wouldn't be faith! By the end of the study, participants will:

- Understand the difference between fairness and justice
- Learn about personal rights and conflict resolution
- Understand what God's image has to do with self-image
- Assess for themselves which research is producing ethical medical therapies
- Understand the abortion debate and learn to help others choose life
- Consider how a biblical worldview has no room for social engineering
- Learn to advocate on behalf of those who are endangered by the eugenics movement
- Grasp a practical handle on complicated end-of-life issues
- Recognize signs of conspicuous consumption in their own lives
- Grasp key principles in welcoming all people in their church

In this introductory session, were participants comfortable with the content and direction of this study? Were they challenged and excited about learning more on the issues? Did other topics that can be researched and addressed (as time permits) surface?

Recommended Resources

Joni Eareckson Tada, *A Lifetime of Wisdom: Embracing the Way God Heals You* (Grand Rapids, MI: Zondervan, 2009).

Dr. Henry Cloud and Dr. John Townsend, *Boundaries: When to Say Yes, How to Say No* (Grand Rapids, MI: Zondervan, 2006).

Helpful Websites

Focus on the Family Citizen Link: www.citizenlink.org
The Manhattan Declaration: www.manhattandeclaration.org

DISCUSSION QUESTIONS

Question 1: Where do you turn to get the news? How do you interpret what you read or watch?

Question 2: Has anyone ever asked you what you believe about one of these issues?

_____ Violence

_____ Autism

_____ Self-Image

_____ Stem Cell Research

_____ Abortion

_____ Genocide

_____ Life Worth

_____ Materialism

Rate the topics in this study using the following scale:

1. I don't think much about it.
2. It is somewhat important to me.
3. I know people who are coping with it.
4. It keeps me awake at night.

Question 3: Do you believe that God's Word provides truth and answers to all these questions?

Question 4: Even the lives of followers of Christ can get out of balance at times. How do you handle this when it happens?

Question 5: Steve told Joni, "God permits what He hates to accomplish what He loves." Have you ever witnessed a time when this happened to someone?

Question 6: How would you define an ethical dilemma?

Question 7: How are our culture's ethical debates putting the health of our communities and families at risk?

Question 8: How can the Church be a force for change when our society is at stake?

WHEN LIFE ISN'T FAIR: VIOLENCE IN THE STREETS

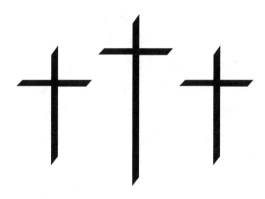

Jesus said, "Father, forgive them, for they do not know what they are doing."
And they divided up his clothes by casting lots.

LUKE 23:34

Life-Coach Leaders

Jesus Christ's crucifixion is perhaps the most extreme example of unfair treatment in life. Yet Jesus prayed for His offenders, even as He took His last breath. He did not harbor unforgiveness or resent His wrongful death; rather, He asked for forgiveness for His murderers' sins. Christ left us an example to emulate, even in death. While reading this chapter, participants will likely remember a story about injustice in their own lives. The cold reality is that we live in a sinful world where life isn't fair and it never will be. How we respond to injustice and unfairness is what matters.

Although most everyone has been treated unjustly at one time or another, few of us can relate to the degree of unfairness revealed in the story of Vicky Olivas. Her story will challenge our preconceived notions about righteous indignation and forgiveness. As participants reflect on injustice, they may realize some of their own old wounds have festered into bitterness. We tend to nurse old wounds. We fantasize about revenge, we harbor unforgiveness, and then we justify our actions. That supposed justification comes from the fact that oftentimes we feel entitled to a reckoning. Many of us cling to our offense, thinking we will forgive when we receive an apology and when remorse is shown. In the meantime, however, we only hurt ourselves by holding on to unforgiveness. There may never be an apology, and the person may not ever feel an ounce of remorse.

So how long will we hold on to the hurt when it's only keeping us in bondage? Some people have gone to their graves clinging to bitterness, while others, like Vicky, have chosen freedom. This study may bring some group members to a crossroads: Will they continue to be chained to the perpetrator of sexual, physical or mental abuse, or to the person who cheated them out of their life savings, or to the individual who hurt their feelings in some way? Or will they break free from the bondage? God's Word is clear if we'll have ears to hear it: "Get rid of all bitterness, rage and anger, brawling and slander, along with every form of malice. Be kind and compassionate to one another, forgiving each other, just as in Christ God forgave you" (Eph. 4:31-32).

What Are the Session Objectives?

In this session on violence, participants will . . .

- Recognize that harboring hurts and offenses only prevents the victim from living an abundant life
- Realize that although we all experience degrees of pain and injustice, it's our reaction that is critical
- Conclude that forgiving another's offenses is not about setting the offender free but about setting one's self free

Why Should Participants Care?

George Herbert once said, "He that cannot forgive others, breaks the bridge over which he himself must pass if he would ever reach heaven; for everyone has need to be forgiven." The root of bitterness and unforgiveness is like a cancer that can eat away at us. Harboring offenses not only keeps us in bondage to the person who offended us, but more importantly, it can keep us from having our own sins forgiven. "For if you forgive men when they sin against you, your heavenly Father will also forgive you. But if you do not forgive men their sins, your Father will not forgive your sins" (Matt. 6:14-15).

Forgiveness is a fundamental principle of the Christian faith. When Jesus was instructing the disciples on how to pray, His exemplary prayer included: "Forgive us our debts, as we also have forgiven our debtors" (Matt. 6:12). This line implies that our being forgiven by God is predicated upon our ability to forgive others. We must embrace this difficult virtue in order to grow in our faith, knowing that we are forgiven and able to forgive others. From Joseph's example of continuing to trust God though he was wronged by his own brothers, to Peter offering to forgive seven times and being told to forgive 77 times, the Bible is chock-full of lessons in forgiveness (see Gen. 37:23-28; Matt. 18:21-22).

Life in Real Time: Violence in the Streets

There's much debate about whether our society has actually gotten more violent, or if our 24-hour news cycle and caught-on-tape frenzy have brought it to the forefront. Either way, the statistics are shocking:

- Every two minutes, someone in the U.S. is sexually assaulted.[1]
- There are more than 1 million gang members in the U.S.[2]
- Almost five children die every day as a result of child abuse.[3]
- Half of the 3.5 million violent crimes in families are committed against a spouse.[4]
- Between 1 and 2 million American seniors have been injured or exploited by someone on whom they depended for protection.[5]
- In 2006, more than one-third of serious violent crimes perpetrated against youth (ages 12 to 18) took place at or on the way to school.[6]
- People with developmental disabilities are 6 times more likely to be victims of crime than other people.[7]

Some people insist that violence is becoming more prevalent because of the disintegration of the family unit. Others point to violent movies and video games or to the growing disregard for civil law as the culprit. Some even say it's bred into the American mindset of radical individualism. Little wonder it's a subject under so much intense scrutiny by sociologists and psychologists.

David Powlison of the Christian Counseling Education Foundation says that when we believe anger is something inside of us—rather than something we actually *do*—then we cannot effectively deal with it.[8] Anger is an honest expression of character. Much like pain, it's an indication that something is amiss and must be dealt with.

In Matthew 18 we see an example of choosing to forgive. A man owed a huge debt to his master. The master was about to have him thrown into prison when the man fell on his knees and begged forgiveness of the debt. The master took pity on him, forgave the debt and sent the man on his way. When that same man saw a friend who owed him a small amount of money but couldn't pay it, he took no pity on the friend and instead had him thrown into prison until he could repay the debt. The master heard about the man's lack of pity and was appalled by his behavior. The master had the man thrown into prison to be tortured until he could repay his own huge debt. The last verse confirms that God wants us to forgive whatever grievances we have against another, because nothing could compare to the debt we've been forgiven through Christ (see Matt. 18:23-35).

By learning and applying Scripture, participants can be set free from a life of bondage to live a life of freedom through forgiveness. Some may share stories of incredible injustice, explaining why they can't let go. Remember that God's Word applies to every circumstance. It could be the first time this person is sharing his or her story publicly. Be sensitive to each person's needs and listen to anyone who wants to open up in that way. It can be incredibly healing to pull a secret out and into the light.

Everyone in the group will likely be able to share a story of unjust, unfair treatment and the anger that resulted. Encourage participation as it may help some group members realize that they're not alone, and they may even be able to recognize their own bitterness. Some might garner hope from another participant's story of forgiveness after harsh treatment. This discussion can be the catalyst to start the members on the road to healing.

You will also need to be mindful of time constraints. You may want to meet with individuals separately, or point them to your pastor, or give them your church's list of recommended Christian counselors and therapists. Make sure each participant's openness is met with love and concern and taken very seriously by all class members.

Consider reading and recommending additional Scriptures on this topic:

- **Jeremiah 29:11:** God has a plan for each of us, which includes a great hope and future.
- **Matthew 5:9:** We all want to be called sons of God.
- **Matthew 5:13:** We want to retain our saltiness.
- **John 10:10:** Unforgiveness steals, kills, and destroys our lives.
- **Romans 12:19:** God will take care of our vengeance.

Leader Checklist

- ❑ Bibles
- ❑ News headlines on violence
- ❑ Copies of the session 2 discussion questions
- ❑ DVD keyed to session 2, "When Life Isn't Fair"
- ❑ Paper and pens

OVERVIEW

Welcome and Opening Prayer

Greet each participant and make him or her feel welcome. Since this is the second session of the course, introduce any new members of the group. Open with prayer, thanking God for bringing each participant back, and calling on His Spirit to reveal any areas of unforgiveness and bitterness.

Opening Activity

Pass out copies of news headlines on violence. Give each member a copy of session 2 discussion questions (see page 53), and then ask the group the first discussion question to help break the ice and get group members focused on this week's topic of violence.

Discussion Question #1
When you think of violent crimes, what top news stories come to mind?

Answers will include personal reflections and opinions—there are no wrong answers.

Discussion Question #2
How do these stories make you feel?

Answers may include sad, angry, helpless, frustrated and/or scared.

Introduction to "When Life Isn't Fair" on the *Life in the Balance* DVD

Briefly tell the group that today's video is about an extremely courageous woman. Vicky Olivas was a young single mother with an 18-month-old son, trying to find a good job to make ends meet. A temporary agency sent her on a job interview that sounded like a wonderful opportunity but ended up turning her life upside down. Today you'll get a firsthand look at her tragedy and her God-honoring response. Show the session 2 segment on the *Life in the Balance* DVD.

Life in the Word

Help the group understand that even though we know that God is sovereign and in control of everything, it can still be easy to point the blame at Him, questioning why He lets bad things happen to good people. Anger toward God can creep in when we feel we've been treated unjustly. Joni says anger at God is almost always sinful, because it's usually a muddle of malice and mistrust about who we think He is.

Fundamentally, we want life to be fair. We want people to treat us fairly. But that is just not the world we live in, and Jesus forewarned us about this when He said, "In this world you will have trouble" (John 16:33). Often the trouble Jesus alerted us to comes at the hands of other people over whom we have no control, people who have been raised in and conditioned by a society filled with violence, people who care nothing about bridling their passions, people who have no resources to deal with anger, people for whom civility and behavioral restraint are foreign concepts.

Discussion Question #3
Have you ever been angry with God? How did you work through your anger?

Make sure the participants grasp the fact that God is a peacemaker and desires for us to live in peace with one another. We should be slow to anger. God desires righteousness, and anger doesn't produce righteousness. Although there are times we cannot avoid the natural response to become angry, how we choose to express that anger is what matters to God. Ask a group member to read aloud Ephesians 4:26, Hebrews 12:14-16 and James 1:19-20. In light of these verses, ask group members to consider discussion question #4.

Discussion Question #4
How should we handle anger toward someone who has hurt us?

Allow time for group members to share their experiences with handling anger. Their responses may include attempts to stuff it inside themselves, harbor bitterness, seek revenge, pray and/or talk to friends. Compare these responses to what God's Word says, keeping in mind that handling anger is difficult and takes practice.

Recall with the group the powerful moment in Vicky's story when she recounted the day the investigators brought her shooter into her hospital room for her to identify. As he stood at the end of her bed, she remembered the Lord asking her, "Are you going to forgive him or not?" Vicky knew at that moment she must choose forgiveness. Only God can perform such a miracle. She believed God's Word, and her godly choice took away a lifetime of burdensome anger and pain toward her perpetrator.

Remind the members that Christians are held to a different standard than the rest of the world. Jesus exhorts us to love our enemies:

Love your enemies and pray for those who persecute you, that you may be sons of your Father in heaven. He causes his sun to rise on the evil and the good, and sends rain on the righteous and the unrighteous. If you love those who love you, what reward will you get? Are not even the tax collectors doing that? And if you greet only your brothers, what are you doing more than others? Do not even pagans do that? (Matt. 5:43-47).

Ask a group member to read Matthew 6:14-15 and Romans 5:3. Allow time for group members to share how harboring anger can affect their lives.

Achieving Personal Balance

Refer to the part of Vicky's story on the DVD when she knew that she had been harboring a deep, seething anger against the man who had attempted to rape her. For many months she had been focusing on *his* sin. However, her anger was an expression of sin having sway in her *own* life. Her quiet rage wasn't righteous in God's eyes, and she had a choice to make. But it wasn't easy.

Explain to the group that anger at God, handled rightly, presents a wonderful opportunity to understand our own heart: First, when we suffer injustice, God has *not* let us down. Nowhere in the Bible do we find a shred of evidence that the Lord ever betrays us. People may betray us, and the devil may torment us, but God neither betrays nor torments us.

Second, we deceive ourselves when we think life should be fair. It's not. And it never will be on this side of eternity. Yet God's Word tells us that His plans are *not* to harm us (or treat us unfairly) but to give us hope and a future (see Jer. 29:11). If we truly believe this, anger at Him will dissolve.

Third, when we place ourselves on the throne of our heart—a throne reserved for the Lord of the universe—our personal rights become the end-all, be-all. We insist we have the right to be respected, to be understood, to have life go our way. When we are *not* respected and understood by family, friends or coworkers—when things don't go *our* way—then we feel violated. That violation breeds anger. And anger unchecked begets violence.

It all comes down to how we relate to God. When we place Jesus Christ on the throne of our hearts and yield our personal rights to Him, purposing to trust Him for whatever happens, we experience true freedom. It takes the supernatural grace of Almighty God to do that, but it's exactly what He provides!

Have someone in the group read Philippians 2:13. Discuss how when it comes to responding in a godly manner to unfair situations, as well as to hurtful people, God's grace is available and abundant to each of us. In fact, as we see in Philippians 2:13, when the Lord gives His grace, He's providing both the *desire* and the *power* to do His will.

Discussion Question #5
What are the characteristics of a person who is harboring bitterness?

Allow time for members to share one-word descriptions of this kind of person. Responses may include aggressive, backbiting and/or self-righteous.

State that when we view our troubles through the lens of eternal glory, we get a different perspective. Troubles are only light when you compare them to something weightier. Keeping an eternal perspective far outweighs our earthly troubles and sorrows.

Explain to the group that if anyone has been struggling with bitter thoughts toward a person who has deeply hurt him or her, there are four important steps to recovery:

1. Forgiveness involves a positive attitude toward the offense rather than a negative attitude toward the offender.
2. Forgiveness views the offender as a tool in God's hands.
3. Forgiveness recognizes that bitterness is assuming a right we don't have.
4. Forgiveness involves cooperating with God for the benefit of others.

Ask different volunteers to read Luke 23:34, Romans 12:19 and 2 Corinthians 4:17, and then ask discussion question #6.

Discussion Question #6
Can you see any positive results from your sufferings? If not, can you still trust God that eternity will outweigh your sufferings? Why or why not?

Ask a volunteer in the group to briefly share a positive example.

Remind participants that others are watching to see how we deal with unfairness and suffering in our lives. As Christians, we have an opportunity to point them to God by living victoriously day after day. Discuss some ways our suffering can point others to Christ. Point out that Joni was bitter and angry when she was first paralyzed, feeling as if God had allowed a great injustice. But now, Joni reflects back to say, "After living more than four decades in a wheelchair, I can honestly say that I would rather be in my chair *knowing* Him than be on my feet without Him."

Discussion Question #7

*Is there someone you don't want to forgive? How does forgiveness
for this person now look in light of God's Word?*

Have members share their personal responses. Again, there are no right or wrong answers.

Tell the group that God is looking for people who will demonstrate true Christian love and mercy, one person at a time—one neighbor, one classmate, one relative, one coworker. He wants His people to be "the salt of the earth," providing a preserving influence for good in our society (Matt. 5:13). He longs for His followers to be "the light of the world," convicting and convincing a hostile culture that peace is the better way (Matt. 5:14).

Read Colossians 3:13. Pass out paper and pens and lead group members to complete one of the following activities, depending on how much time there is available:

Option A: Invite participants to write a letter to someone they need to forgive. Encourage them to include all the things they want to say and then take the letter home with them and throw it away or burn it.

Option B: Challenge participants to write out their entire story with all the details that have been hidden. Then, as a symbol of forgiveness, tell them to lift their story up to God as they prayerfully give it all to Him. This exercise can be monumental as they believe God will take hold of the pain and deal with it on their behalf. Suggest that they take the story home with them and burn it, so there is never any fear of it being found.

Balancing Faith and Culture

Point out to the group that our culture has taught us that it's okay to harbor unforgiveness toward someone who has wronged us or that someone needs to make restitution for his or her offense before we can let it go. Scripture tells us something very different. Forgiveness is woven into the fabric of both the Old and New Testaments. As we've seen throughout this study, we only hurt ourselves when we cling to bitterness and unforgiveness.

Explain to the group that the word "atone" means to make amends or reparation, as for an offense or a crime. Going all the way back to Leviticus, we find that God knew human beings must forgive and be forgiven (see Lev. 23:26-28). Many in the Jewish culture still observe a Day of Atonement, or Yom Kippur, when they reflect on reconciling with both God and neighbor. Just prior to Yom Kippur, Jews will ask forgiveness of those they have wronged during the prior year (if they have not already done so). On the day itself, Jews fast and pray for God's forgiveness for the transgressions they have made against Him throughout the year. Yom Kippur, which means Day of Atonement in Hebrew, is the holiest day of the year in the Jewish calendar.

Closing Prayer

Take a moment to reflect through prayer on God's special care and provision for each of us. Thank Him for His truth that sets people free from unforgiveness. Pray for the men and women who may still be struggling with this issue.

Pray for those who have committed violent crimes.

Pray to be forgiven as we forgive others.

Pray for those who suffer injustice and yet continue to live lives that point people to Christ.

Pray for an eternal perspective.

Pray that this study of violence and forgiveness has provided an opportunity for the participants to embrace the forgiveness we have through Jesus Christ and to reflect that same forgiveness to a hurting world, one person at a time.

Evaluating the Session

Were the session objectives met? Did participants understand how forgiveness is freeing and how unforgiveness is bondage?

Was each participant able to identity someone he or she needed to forgive, and was that participant able to apply God's forgiveness?

Was there anyone who seemed to struggle with this session, someone who might need additional prayers and follow-up this week?

Recommended Resources

R.T. Kendall, *Total Forgiveness* (Lake Mary, FL: Charisma House, 2002).

Nancy Leigh DeMoss, *Choosing Forgiveness: Your Journey to Freedom* (Chicago, IL: Moody Publishers, 2008).

Helpful Websites

Practicing Our Faith, The Practices: Forgiveness: http://www.practicingourfaith.org/prct_forgiveness.html

About.com: Christianity: http://christianity.about.com/od/whatdoesthebiblesay/a/bible forgivenes.htm

SESSION 2

DISCUSSION QUESTIONS

Question 1: When you think of violent crimes, what top news stories come to mind?

Question 2: How do these stories make you feel?

Question 3: Have you ever been angry with God? How did you work through your anger?

Question 4: How should we handle anger toward someone who has hurt us?

Question 5: What are the characteristics of a person who is harboring bitterness?

Question 6: Can you see any positive results from your sufferings? If not, can you still trust God that eternity will outweigh your sufferings? Why or why not?

Question 7: Is there someone you don't want to forgive? How does forgiveness for this person now look in light of God's Word?

MAKING SENSE OF AUTISM

Jesus said, "Let the little children come to me, and do not hinder them,
for the kingdom of heaven belongs to such as these."

MATTHEW 19:14

Life-Coach Leaders

Maybe you know of families affected by autism, whose lives are completely overwhelmed by the challenges they now face. You want to embrace them as brothers and sisters in Christ, but you simply don't know how to help. Or you may be wary of associating with them simply because you've been misinformed or have come to believe some common myths associated with a diagnosis of autism. Think about a time when you have felt misunderstood. Perhaps a friend took the wrong way a comment you made or a coworker misquoted you in a meeting. Now imagine having a child with a disability that is so ambiguous that people actually point fingers at you—the parent!

What Are the Session Objectives?

In this session on autism, participants will . . .

- Learn the common myths that accompany autism
- Understand important and unique family dynamics

- Grasp key principles to help churches welcome individuals with autism and their families

Why Should Participants Care?

Autism is growing at epidemic proportions. The journal *Pediatrics* reports that 1 percent of U.S. children ages 3 to 17 have an autism spectrum disorder. That means about 1 in every 91 children. This is a dramatic increase from the 1 in 150 rate more commonly reported.[1]

Participants in your group will have had various exposures to autism. Some may have a family member or friend with autism or work as a special educator or therapist. Others have never met anyone with the disorder, but if they are media savvy, they may relate to movie portrayals of autism such as in *Rain Man, Forrest Gump* and *I Am Sam*. And a growing number of family sitcoms on television include children with autism.

Throughout this session, encourage participants to show Christ-like compassion toward families coping with autism and to build lasting relationships that are mutually beneficial and that build God's kingdom.

DVD Options

Decide ahead of time how best to use the DVD for your particular group. Preview the videos with your small group's interests in mind. Then select one of these viewing options to use during this session as time permits:

Option A: View the first 15 minutes of part 1 and the last 15 minutes of Part 2.

Option B: Ask the participants to consider making this a two-week session, viewing parts 1 and 2 on consecutive weeks.

Option C: Encourage participants to sign up to borrow the DVDs for home viewing, including the special features, which offer insights for those serving children with autism in churches or communities.

"Making Sense of Autism" Outline

This two-part series contains two 30-minute DVDs plus two special-feature interviews with experts in the field of autism. Part 1 explains the four common myths about autism:

Myth 1: We know the causes and cures for autism.
Myth 2: All people with autism have mental retardation.

Myth 3: All people with autism behave the same.

Myth 4: Autism is caused by poor parenting.

Part 2 explains the truths about autism for the Church:

Truth 1: Autism separates families from the church.

Truth 2: Autism creates fears the Church can ease.

Truth 3: People with autism can know and serve God.

Truth 4: Autism can strengthen faith communities.

Life in Real Time: Learning About Autism

Autism was first described by Leo Kanner of John's Hopkins in 1940 and was applied to individuals who exhibited the following criteria: (1) failure to have normal reciprocal social interactions, (2) impaired language or communication skills, and (3) restricted, stereotyped patterns of interests and activities. These traits may appear as early as 18 months of age or much later, during the elementary years. While genetic links have not been clearly identified, twins are 60 percent to 90 percent more likely to both have autism.[2]

Autism is called a spectrum disorder because it includes a wide range of neurological conditions, from high-functioning savants to low-functioning individuals with multiple disorders. It includes Asperger's syndrome, pervasive developmental disorders (PDD), and Rett syndrome (which can be accompanied by mental disabilities and seizures).

For those participants who want to learn more about working with families coping with autism, recommend that they purchase the complete *Making Sense of Autism* DVDs from Joni and Friends. The DVD set includes special features: In part 1, Dr. Laura Hendrickson, author of *Finding Your Child's Way on the Autism Spectrum*, discusses issues of spiritual growth, parenting and marriage. In part 2, Barbara J. Newman, author of *Autism and Your Church*, offers expert advice on how your church can welcome and include children with autism and their families.

Leader Checklist

- ❑ Bibles
- ❑ News headlines on autism
- ❑ Copies of session 3 discussion questions
- ❑ DVD keyed to session 3, "Making Sense of Autism"

OVERVIEW

Welcome and Opening Prayer

Welcome participants and open the session with prayer, asking God to open their hearts and minds for understanding as you present this topic on understanding autism.

Opening Activity

Before you introduce the topic, ask the participants to consider the following scenario:

You and your children are excited about taking homemade cookies to your new neighbors, who appear to have a child the same age as your son, Tim. A frazzled young mother welcomes you in and introduces you to her son, David, who is struggling to escape out the front door. When he is told to stop and sit down, he screams no and starts banging his head against the wall.

Ask the participants to indicate by the number of fingers they hold up which of the following answers describes what they would do:

1. Tell her that you've obviously caught them at a bad time and quickly usher your children home, explaining that David is obviously a troubled child.
2. Tell her that you can come back later, knowing you won't, because you don't want Tim or any of your children exposed to such unruly behavior.
3. Go home and call the church prayer group to remember this stressed-out family in their prayers.
4. Ignore David's behavior as his mom deals with him and wait for an opportunity to tell her that you're happy to meet her and David.

Participants will answer differently based on whether or not they have read the chapter. However, if most of them were honest, they probably picked one of the first three answers.

Explain that David's mother was not surprised by his behavior, and she may have just needed a moment to calm him down. She may (or may not) have offered an explanation, which is okay. It is almost certain that she would have appreciated a kind gesture, even if she felt embarrassed for a moment.

Hand out news headlines on autism, and briefly discuss the focus of each headline. Then give each member a copy of session 3 discussion questions (see page 69) and ask the group the first discussion question.

Discussion Question #1

Why is it so tempting to judge parents by their children's behaviors?
What does that say about human nature?

Allow time for participants to briefly share their responses, then point out that most parents feel inadequate at one time or another. If a friend's child uses perfect manners, we wonder why our children can't be like that. But if a child has a temper tantrum, we swell with pride, thinking our child knows how to act in public. It is human nature to criticize behaviors that we don't understand, but God clearly tells us to avoid judging others.

Read Galatians 6:3-5 and James 4:11, and then ask members to share what advice these verses give about judging others' behavior.

Discussion Question #2

How would you react if there were no cure for a disorder
that your child or loved one was facing?

Allow time for members to respond. Answers may include worried, anxious, afraid, angry and/or desperate. Explain how parents generally deal with problems: Fathers are big on fixing things. They want to examine the problem, collect the data, discuss the options and find a solution! Mothers, with tissue boxes under their arms, tend to talk, feed and cuddle the problem until it simply goes away.

When the problem is as enormous as autism spectrum disorder, however, responses vary considerably. Many parents roll up their sleeves and make sweeping lifestyle changes to help their children succeed. Their love and courage won't allow them to give up. They don't feel like heroes, but they are. Other parents are left with haunting guilt and confusion and have no idea what to do or even whom to ask for help. In other situations, children with autism are being raised in the foster-care system, where conditions are too often less than ideal.

Read Proverbs 3:5-6 and 1 Corinthians 13:12. Explain that parenting can be a treacherous journey of learning to trust God with our children's lives, believing that His plans for them are perfect.

Introduction to "Making Sense of Autism" on the *Life in the Balance* DVD

Today's video will introduce your group to families who are bravely navigating the complicated world of autism. Their stories of utter frustration and tender joy reveal their dependence on a loving God. The group will also hear from several experts in the field of autism who are passionate about equipping churches to reach out and embrace families living with this puzzling disorder.

While every day more and more children are being diagnosed with autism, the causes of autism remain unknown and a cure has yet to be found. In addition to the uncertainties about the future, families affected by autism face a number of misunderstandings about autism, such as the myth that these children can't learn and that their poor behavior is caused by a lack of discipline. This session also discusses the role of the Church in the lives of families affected by autism, as well as the blessings that come from including every person in the Body of Christ.

Show the portions of session 3 that you pre-selected on the *Life in the Balance* DVD.

Life in the Word

As participants reflect on what they have seen in the video, invite them to respond with *one word* that sums up their thoughts. Answers may include saddened, overwhelmed, unaware, inspired and/or challenged. Then ask the third discussion question.

Discussion Question #3

If you had a child with autism, how might your family's weekly activities change?

Let group members briefly share their responses. Point out to the group that today's families are bombarded with activity options for children of all ages. Parents camp out for days to register their children in the best schools. They carry Blackberries and iPods that contain color-coded schedules for each child's game, lesson, recital, party and sleepover. In some neighborhoods, kids' allowances are at an all-time high and include personal credit cards.

A diagnosis of autism changes everything, especially in terms of time and money, especially when children are lower functioning or have multiple diagnoses. Parents have little time for themselves and often fight exhaustion. Siblings may have to limit their activities when family budgets are stretched by high medical costs. The whole family can feel stressed and isolated.

Read Psalm 142:4 and Ecclesiastes 4:9-12. Explain that this is why church programs are so important; special-needs ministries connect these families with those who care enough to come alongside and help lift their load. Ask group members to now consider discussion question #4.

Discussion Question #4
If you spent the day with a child with autism, what might be the most challenging thing for you?

Allow time for members to respond. Individual responses to this question will be influenced by each participant's personality type and by his or her experience as a parent. This question will give participants insight into their own feelings about children with autism.

Read Luke 9:46-48 and James 2:1-8. This may be a good time to challenge participants to consider volunteering to serve children with special needs at church or at a local respite (rest) program. A growing number of churches offer respite programs where parents drop their children off for three or four hours of quality care and planned activities. Moms and dads can then go to dinner, walk in the park, shop or just rest! It's also a great help to single parents, as divorce is a sad result of the toll autism can take on families.

Discussion Question #5
How would you respond to someone who says that caring for children with autism is the job of the government, not the Church?

Point out to the group that families affected by autism live in neighborhoods near your church. Read Matthew 28:19-20. The Great Commission sends us out to make disciples of *all* people, teaching them to obey Christ's commands. Dr. Scott Daniels is a senior pastor in Southern California at a church that has a thriving special-needs ministry. "We misunderstand Christ's mandate when we allow the government to take the Church's role," says Dr. Daniels. "We lose so much of who we are as the Body of Christ. We're people called to be salt and light in the world." While social services can help families affected by autism, these services can never lead a child to Christ. However, when we go in Jesus' name, we can introduce a whole family to our Lord and Savior.

Achieving Personal Balance

Begin by asking if any of the participants have ever felt painfully alone in a crowded room. If so, then he or she can relate to families struggling with autism. They feel obscured behind a wall of autism when what they desire most is simply to fit in.

Tell the group about Sarah Stup, a 24-year-old woman with autism who is nonverbal and struggles with repetitive behaviors. Read this excerpt from Sarah's book *Are Your Eyes Listening?* in which she expresses her need to be accepted:

> I am inside. The words are there; the voice is not.
> It is lonely and sad not to talk.
> We who are silent have our value.
> Being autistic is a battle that stays.
> Your world hurts me.
> Sounds pay me visits after I leave them.
> I need autism to breathe.
> Autism is awful, but I am not awful.
> I act dumb, but am smart. Please be my friend.
> We can't be friends when you hate autism.
> Be an explorer who finds treasures beyond the strangeness.[3]

Sarah wants us to know that autism is part of a shield that she and others like her need. Without it, she wouldn't be who she is. Tell participants that if they are interested in reading more of Sarah's work, they should visit her website at www.SarahStup.com.

Explain to the group that thanks to new therapies and technologies, people with autism who are nonverbal are now able to express their thoughts. Imagine a mom's amazement when her son types "I love you, Mom!" on a computer screen for the first time, opening up a new world of communication. Ask participants what it would take for them to open their hearts to the possibility that children and adults with autism can strengthen their faith as well as the fiber of their church. Allow a moment for one or two members to respond, and then ask your group to consider discussion question #6.

Discussion Question #6

What qualities did you see in the parents in the video that you
want to emulate in your own life?

Let participants briefly share their observations. Answers may include determination, courage, dedication, love and/or hope.

Read Galatians 5:22-23 and Philippians 3:12-14. Explain that the importance of embracing families affected by autism has been made clear, but there is also a lot we can learn from them. Dr. Jeff McNair, who teaches adults with developmental disabilities at his church, says, "These families teach us how to love other people. If someone comes to me with poor social skills and I reject him, I've sinned—he didn't. So if the Lord brings people into my life who are socially incompetent to teach me, then that is a benefit." When we act with the mind of Christ, we have a tremendous opportunity to grow alongside of these families. At whatever age a child is diagnosed with autism, our response should be: "We don't care what your child's disability is; there's a place for you here." This goes beyond just providing child care so that families can worship; it also means helping the entire family fully participate in our fellowship.

Discussion Question #7

Have your perceptions about individuals with autism changed after viewing these videos? In what ways?

Allow a few volunteers to share changes that have occurred. Comment that when you see beyond the diagnosis of autism, you can embrace these children as God's unique creations. Only then can you offer them acceptance and true empathy. When the children display inappropriate behaviors, you will understand that they are not bad children. You will learn that spending time with them will require a little advance preparation and lots of flexibility, and you will understand that the key is to be faithful and consistent, knowing that tough days require patience and love.

Have a volunteer read Proverbs 22:6 and James 2:20-22,26. Point out that experts remind us that children with autism are visual learners: "If they didn't see it, you didn't say it."[4] The same can be said of faith! If people can't see it, what we say doesn't matter.

Balancing Faith and Culture

Remind the group that Christian friends can make a huge difference in the lives of children and adults with autism. For many of us this will require a major shift in our thinking, but the transformation can bring glory to God and a fresh maturity to the Church. For example, if we think that individuals with autism can't understand spiritual things, we'll miss the joy of teaching them about God. If we think that they only want to be cared for, we won't experience the blessings that their love and service can bring into our own lives.

The first step is to recognize how our message must contrast with the message of the world. With the group, go over the differences between the secular worldview of children with autism and the biblical worldview of the same children. You could tell the secular worldview and let the group respond with the biblical view.

SECULAR WORLDVIEW OF CHILDREN WITH AUTISM	BIBLICAL WORLDVIEW OF CHILDREN WITH AUTISM
We can't change the program for just one child.	Every member of the Body of Christ is equally important.
Special education is okay, as long as it doesn't affect my child.	My child needs to learn compassion for those with special needs.
We've all got our own problems.	As we draw near to those in need, God draws near to us.

(Participants may have other observations to add to this list.)

The apostle Paul makes our mission clear in Romans 12:5: "In Christ we, though many, form one body, and each member belongs to all the others" (*TNIV*). Nothing is more beautiful than to see a mature church fully functioning as Christ planned—and that includes children and adults with autism.

Discussion Question #8

What would practical support from your church look like for these families affected by autism?

Allow time for group members to respond. Next, share with the group that they may be surprised to find an ad like the following one in their local newspaper. It shows how today's savvy marketers are tapping into the needs of families coping with autism:

Special Screening for Special Needs . . . The Autism Society and AMC Entertainment continues the Sensory Friendly Films series at participating AMC theaters. Kids with special needs can get up, walk around and make noises as needed. No previews or advertisements will be shown before the movie, the lights will be brought up and the sound turned down, and families can bring their own snacks for the movie.

Read Romans 15:5-7. Point out that God's Word says that our acceptance of others brings praise to God. God often uses one family to spark a vision for a special-needs ministry. Joni and Friends often gets notes like the following one from a pastor: "Parents bring children with autism to our church, and we don't know what to do with them." The organization's response includes providing a list of resources such as the *Special Needs Smart Pages* by Joni and Friends, which is packed with how-to articles and program options. Joni and Friends also recommends partnering with churches and organizations that have special classes, parent support groups, sibling events, health fairs, and family camps. Tell the group that many resources are listed on the Joni and Friends website at www.joniandfriends.org.

Closing Prayer

As you conclude, ask if participants know of individuals with autism. If possible, create a prayer list using the first name of each individual. Encourage participants to make personal contact with those families.

Pray that children with autism will discover that for every weakness they have, God has given them a corresponding strength.

Pray that families affected by autism will keep their eyes on Christ, trusting that with the right attitude, His glory can be revealed, even in difficult circumstances.

Pray that more churches will determine to include these families in their family of faith.

Evaluating the Session

Were the session objectives met? Did the discussion questions reveal needs in the hearts of the participants? Did the Scriptures lead participants to new attitudes toward children with autism? Do participants know of families affected by autism that your group can serve in some way?

Recommended Resources

Barbara J. Newman, *Autism and Your Church: Nurturing the Spiritual Growth of People with Autism Spectrum Disorders* (Grand Rapids, MI: Faith Alive Christian Resource & Friendship Ministries, 2006).

Barbara J. Newman, *Helping Kids Include Kids with Disabilities* (Grand Rapids, MI: CRC Publications, 2001).

Joni and Friends, *Special Needs Smart Pages: Advice, Answers and Articles About Ministering to Children with Special Needs* (Ventura, CA: Regal, 2009).

Joni and Friends, *The Father's House: Welcoming and Including People and Families Affected by Disability* (DVD) (Agoura Hills, CA: Joni and Friends, 2007).

Helpful Websites

Ability Online: www.ablelink.org

CLC Network: www.clcnetwork.org

Friendship Ministries: www.friendship.org

National Autism Association: www.nationalautismassociation.org

DISCUSSION QUESTIONS

Question 1: Why is it so tempting to judge parents by their children's behaviors? What does that say about human nature?

Question 2: How would you react if there were no cure for a disorder that you or your loved one was facing?

Question 3: If you had a child with autism, how might your family's weekly activities change?

Question 4: If you spent the day with a child with autism, what might be the most challenging thing for you?

Question 5: How would you respond to someone who says that caring for children with autism is the job of the government, not the Church?

Question 6: What qualities did you see in the parents in the video that you want to emulate in your own life?

Question 7: Have your perceptions about individuals with autism changed after viewing this video? In what ways?

Question 8: What would practical support from your church look like for families affected by autism?

SELF-IMAGE IN A FICKLE CULTURE

For we are God's workmanship, created in Christ Jesus to do good works,
which God prepared in advance for us to do.

EPHESIANS 2:10

Life-Coach Leaders

Over the last few decades, our society has increased the pressure to achieve an unattainable concept of beauty. Thanks to modern editing software, we're bombarded by images of women who in actuality bear little resemblance to their selves in print. Ads like the Dove Campaign for Real Beauty and news articles exposing the extent of retouching in the everyday image industry bring this pressure into focus.[1] Young girls are especially susceptible to the lies each false image perpetuates, but many adults are also unable to escape the allure.

Constant marketing messages feed dissatisfaction and push new products, procedures or programs. This not only affects a person's perspective of his or her worth, but it can also lead to questions about God's goodness and sovereignty. Some of our more detestable traits seem to lack the planning of a caring designer. A distrust bred in the realm of personal appearance and abilities inhibits intimacy with the Creator and can stall true intimacy with friends and family. A wife cannot accept that her husband thinks she's beautiful if she feels her reflection belies God's handiwork. Nor will the beauty of his wife satisfy a husband who accepts the false images the world provides.

What Are the Session Objectives?

In this session on self-image, participants will . . .

- Understand how a young person's view of their appearance, abilities, and family background shape their self-concept
- Distinguish the signals of a negative self-image from a healthy self-image
- Understand what the Bible says about accepting one's self in a God-glorifying manner

Why Should Participants Care?

Participants may or may not know how a poor self-image destroys relationships and can prevent a person from loving others. The bondage of comparison lies at the core of an unhealthy self-image. A person may even be unaware of an internal dialogue of how he or she does not measure up. Negative self-talk can saturate thoughts and destroy confidence. Comparisons involving a spouse, children or fellow churchgoers contribute to a greater insecurity in God's design for everyone involved.

Life in Real Time: Self-Image

As Christians, we should be up in arms, rallying around younger generations to help them see the truth. However, we shouldn't be surprised by this age-old tactic. After all, C. S. Lewis discerned the problem in 1942, describing what he called the demonic triumph of the eye in *The Screwtape Letters*. During Lewis's demonic dialogue, the elder demon proposes to make "the role of the eye in sexuality more and more important [while] at the same time making its demands more and more impossible."[2] As Ralph C. Wood states in "The Triumph of the Eye":

When the eye triumphs, especially in the way men view women, then something demonic happens, Lewis suggests. . . . Writing more than sixty years ago, he nonetheless foresaw the familiar pattern of our time. "We now teach men," Screwtape gleefully confirms, "to like women whose bodies are scarcely distinguishable from those of boys." The devils thus prompt women to wear clothes that "make them appear firmer and more slender and more boyish than nature allows a full-grown woman to be. . . . The moral and religious implications here are huge, not only for women, but also for us men who, because we are dominated by the eye, demand that women meet the expectations of the notorious "male gaze."[3]

The prince of this age is constantly bombarding us with messages about beauty, brains, brawn, money and sex. No wonder the Bible warns, "For everything in the world—the cravings of sinful man, the lust of his eyes and the boasting of what he has and does—comes not from the Father but from the world. The world and its desires pass away, but the man who does the will of God lives forever" (1 John 2:16-17).

Unlike some of the other topics in this study, self-image is an area that has almost certainly touched each participant in the group. Each person will likely have some experience with struggles in this area. This may require an extra measure of sensitivity, because some participants may use examples that could unwittingly alienate other members of the group, especially when it comes to cosmetic procedures. Work to allow honest discussion without provoking unnecessary defensive stances.

Leader Checklist

☐ Bibles
☐ News headlines on self-image
☐ Copies of Session 4 Discussion Questions
☐ DVD keyed to session 4, "Self-Image in a Fickle Culture"

OVERVIEW

Welcome and Opening Prayer

Welcome participants and open the session with prayer, asking God to open their hearts and minds for understanding as you present this topic on self-image and today's culture.

Opening Activity

Hand out news headlines on self-image. Ask participants to describe what makes a person beautiful or handsome. Consider having them think of close friends or family members who are beautiful and naming what characteristics contribute to that sense.

You may also wish to host a game-show quiz featuring untouched photos and their enhanced or retouched counterparts. Use examples from your own family photos or print examples found on the Internet (pairs of photos can be found at http://www.campaign forrealbeauty.ca; follow the link "For Girls Only" and select the quiz under "Image Manipulation.") Ask contestants to point out the places that have been altered in some way on the photos. Give each member a copy of session 4 discussion questions (see pages 00-00), and then ask the group the first discussion question.

Discussion Question #1

What aspects often contribute to a person's self-image?

Explain to the group that self-image is defined as "one's conception of oneself or of one's role."[4] A child's family, religious upbringing, and self-discovery first shape the child's self-image. Soon, however, society influences self-image with messages of what the child should be, look like or do. These factors continue to compete for attention throughout a person's life.

Pressure from peers, the media, authority figures, and cultural values and trends can pull a person's self-perception in all directions. Cultural pressures to copy a hairstyle or

75

wear the latest "in" colors are easier to discern because those things change so frequently. Cultural values and trends, which change more slowly, can be harder to detect. Trends pressure us to do such things as wear brown this season or enroll our kids in a particular sport. All of those temporary ideals contribute to our feelings about our worth and purpose, and they also often form the basis of our sense of security. Read 1 Samuel 16:7. Allow time for members to share how this verse says we should look at ourselves and others.

Point out to the group that the story of Naomi in the Old Testament book of Ruth gives us an example of how self-image can be affected by circumstances. Naomi returned to her homeland after the death of her husband and sons. Naomi's name meant "pleasant," but she told everyone to call her a name meaning "bitter" (see Ruth 1:20-21). She chose to establish her identity in a temporary circumstance rather than a permanent reality. She had no way of knowing that she was only at the beginning of the story of God's amazing provision for her.

Ask a member to read Ruth 4:14-16. It should be clear to the participants that Naomi grew old accompanied by the loving devotion of her daughter-in-law, the care of Boaz and the joy of her grandson.

Discussion Question #2
Think of an area about which you have been self-conscious.
How did this make you feel?

Let several members share their personal experiences. Their responses may include lonely, inadequate, anger toward God, and/or the need to prove something. Explain to the participants that a negative self-image can create an inability to trust God. Many people with a negative self-image also indulge in resistance against authority or exhibit an overemphasis on materialism.

There are several examples in Scripture of Moses exhibiting a negative view of himself. Born a child to Hebrew slaves but raised by the daughter of the Egyptian pharaoh, Moses grew up with competing identities. In Exodus 2, Moses murdered an Egyptian to aid a Hebrew slave. His uncertain sense of identity resulted in confusion when he later tried to stop two Hebrews from fighting. The two angry men rejected him and his authority. Years later, Moses even gave his first son a name that meant "an alien in a foreign land" (Exod. 2:22). Moses didn't know where to root his identity.

Decades later, at the burning bush, Moses still felt burdened by his own feelings of inadequacy and insecurity. Read Exodus 3:11-14. Point out to the group that Moses didn't believe God knew best when He told him to go speak to Pharaoh on behalf of the Israelites.

Moses asked, "Who am I, that I should go?" God's response emphasized that His presence alone—nothing else—qualified Moses.

Discussion Question #3

How has a negative view of how you were designed affected your behavior and relationships?

Allow time for participants to respond. Tell the group that many people deflect compliments or thanks and instead answer such kind words by pointing out their flaws or diminishing the value of their work. This discourages honest gratitude, and false humility can push people away.

A teenager may try to hide large pimples with a hovering hand or carefully placed hair. A mother may miss out on family fun at the pool because her bathing suit cover-up doesn't cover enough. A man may work long hours to hide his insecurities about how much he knows. A frustrated housekeeper may not enjoy inviting guests into a less-than-organized home.

Maybe, like Moses, a person has not followed God's call on his or her life because a falsely perceived weakness overwhelms the person. As a measure of self-protection, we may keep friends and family at a distance, because we fear that they will see the weakness we see in ourselves and think less of us for it.

Conclude this section by reading aloud 2 Corinthians 12:9 and Romans 9:20. Allow volunteers to tell what those verses say about self-image.

Introduction to "Self-Image in a Fickle Culture" on the *Life in the Balance* DVD

In today's video, the group will meet Holly Strother, a beautiful young woman with spina bifida. The group will also hear from her parents as they share their initial struggles as they realized their newborn daughter had a birth defect, saying it felt as if God had interrupted their plans. Through the many surgeries and resulting physical challenges of Holly's spina bifida, both she and her parents clung to a hard-won faith. Now, because of what she has experienced and learned, Holly intentionally looks for ways to encourage others who face similar challenges. She doesn't struggle with comparisons, which has allowed her to have an open and nonjudgmental personality. Holly has worked hard to cultivate the beauty God created her to have, not with outward efforts, but by trusting God in the difficult circumstances of her life and focusing on His plans for her rather than beauty tips found in any magazine. Now show the session 4 segment on the *Life in the Balance* DVD.

Life in the Word

Take a few minutes for members to reflect on the video, sharing thoughts and impressions. Then read Hebrews 12:2 and 1 Peter 3:3-4, and ask members to respond to discussion question #4.

Discussion Question #4

What can you do to keep yourself from the destructive habit of making comparisons?

Point out to the group that in the video, Holly shared that she doesn't struggle with comparisons. She knows this confidence enables her to reach out to others. Some solutions for those of us who do struggle may include avoiding certain magazines and television shows that foster dissatisfaction. We can also refuse to engage in conversations that play the comparison game.

Suggest to participants that they memorize verses related to our God-given worth. Tell them that memorization helps to refocus our minds on the things to which we should pay attention. It can also prevent lies about us from having the last say in our thoughts.

Explain that above all, we, like Holly, must focus on Jesus Christ. This involves two aspects. First, we can aim for the qualities He desires us to develop—the fruit of the Spirit as listed in Galatians 5:22-23, the characteristics of love as detailed in 1 Corinthians 13, and the armor of God as explained in Ephesians 6:10-18. According to Galatians 5:23, "Against such things there is no law." The woman or man who grows in these qualities will be attractive to everyone.

The second aspect of focusing on Jesus Christ is to remember His saving work on the cross. Jesus didn't turn from the shame of death on the cross for the sake of the joy of reconciling humankind to God. While Jesus authored and perfected this reconciliation, we can still participate in it. We do this when we scorn shame for the sake of seeing others reconciled to God.

Achieving Personal Balance

Begin this next section by asking the group discussion question #5.

Discussion Question #5

Where does your attention go as you study a piece of art?

Allow time for members to respond. Explain that an artist's medium, technique, use of light, and choice of subject all contribute to the resulting creation. Artwork always draws attention to the skill and purpose of the artist. Regardless of whether the art has stood the test of time or will only hang on a refrigerator door, art speaks about the artist. Even if someone has no knowledge of art appreciation, the dedication and patience required for the Sistine Chapel will likely appear as a marvel to everyone. The artwork brought home in a backpack reflects the interests and perhaps favorite colors of the small artist. The better one knows the artist—his or her thoughts, technique, history and purpose—the more the artwork increases in value (at least to the person who admires it). Still, in most cases, the value of the artwork depends on the skill and reputation of the artist.

Read Genesis 1:26-27,31 and Psalm 139:13-16. Discuss the fact that God designed us and created us. When He finished making humankind, He declared us "very good." We are the work of the most skilled Artist! The more we know the Artist, the more we will appreciate His handiwork.

Discussion Question #6
Have you initially had trouble accepting a circumstance as God's design
only to see later a bigger purpose than you could have imagined?

Allow a few volunteers to answer before telling the group about Gladys Aylward and Amy Carmichael, two women who had this trouble initially. Gladys Aylward, as a young girl, hated her straight black hair and the fact that she never grew taller than four feet ten inches. Not until she arrived in China as a missionary did she see God's greater purpose in the way He had created her. Her dark hair and shorter stature allowed her to blend in among the people she worked with. Her hated characteristics allowed her to have a more effective ministry. Amy Carmichael prayed as a child for blue eyes but learned of God's specific plan for her brown eyes as a missionary in India. Her eyes allowed her better anonymity rescuing girls from temple slavery in that country.

Point out that though not all physical traits have such an obvious purpose, God does carefully plan out each of our physical traits. Read Zephaniah 3:17 and John 9:1-3. A child may receive special comfort from his or her mother's soft lap when no amount of abdominal work could firm it. A wife may enjoy the way her husband's hair curls in precisely the "wrong" way. But above all, God oversees each tiny detail that makes a person uniquely themselves, and He takes delight in the work of His hands.

Balancing Faith and Culture

Help the group understand that a person's true value and worth originate from God. With that in mind, all Christians must be accepting of others (after all, God made us all), but that does not mean we should be accepting of wrong behavior, like that of bullying.

Organizations concerned with various issues are joining efforts against bullying, and the issue comes to the forefront particularly during Bullying Prevention Awareness Week in October. Bullying injures a person's physical health and destroys self-confidence. It is a serious issue and, as Christians, we must discourage it whenever possible. Even in instances where we must disagree with the thoughts, attitudes or actions of another person, we cannot condone bullying.

The Manhattan Declaration addresses this by saying:

> Our rejection of sin, though resolute, must never become the rejection of sinners. For every sinner, regardless of the sin, is loved by God, who seeks not our destruction but rather the conversion of our hearts. Jesus calls all who wander from the path of virtue to "a more excellent way." As his disciples we will reach out in love to assist all who hear the call and wish to answer it.[5]

The Manhattan Declaration also affirms the increased likelihood that courtrooms will prosecute statements of disapproval as hate crimes: "In Canada and some European nations, Christian clergy have been prosecuted for preaching biblical norms against the practice of homosexuality. New hate-crime laws in America raise the specter of the same practice here." Like Peter and John in Acts 4, we must obey God above all.

Discussion Question #7

How can we hold to absolute truths regarding sin and share our convictions without fostering bullying or instigating hate crimes?

Allow time for members to respond, and then read Psalm 138:8 and Ephesians 2:10. Discuss how these passages apply to each person's situation. Point out that the circumstances of a person's ideas and actions do not change the inherent worth God gave when He created the individual. Sin and rebellion can stall the full development of God's blueprint for a person's life, but God is not finished yet.

The participants need to understand that edifying speech affirms the worth of a person. Jokes that put down an individual or a group have no place in Christian speech. We must root out teasing unless clearly acknowledged by both parties as harmless and even beneficial. Our respect for the person we disagree with must be evident despite our disagreement with his or her lifestyle and convictions.

Discussion Question #8

*What additional confidence relating to self-image do people who
have claimed Christ as Savior have?*

Allow time for members to respond, and then explain that self-image involves a desire to belong and be accepted. As new creations in Christ, God has forgiven our sin and we can stand blameless before Him. We *do* belong and we *are* accepted. Our names are written in the Book of Life; and our home, the place we belong, is secure.

Have a volunteer read Romans 8:11,37-39. Help the group realize that God accepts us, not because of our innate qualities or cultivated attributes, but because of what Jesus Christ did on the cross on our behalf. The reconciliation we have with our Creator fulfills our deepest need, our deepest want. Because we are secure in Christ, we have no reason to entertain any insecurities.

Closing Prayer

Invite participants to think specifically of an area of their self-image that they struggle with or that someone they love struggles with. Ask them to pray for these things silently as you close in prayer.

Pray for young people in the Church, so they can discern the lies society tells them about beauty and where to find their worth.

Pray for husbands and wives to trust God with their insecurities and allow for truer intimacy in marriage.

Pray for each participant in the group to speak affirming words into the lives of those around them, enabling others to have a self-image grounded in truth.

Evaluating the Session

Were the session objectives met? Did the discussion questions reveal needs in the hearts of the participants? Did participants reconsider the voices defining beauty in their life? Did participants go away with a fresh understanding of God's design for their life?

Recommended Resources

Tracy Klehn, *Growing Friendship: Connecting More Deeply with Those Who Matter Most* (Grand Rapids, MI: Bethany House, 2007).

Joni Eareckson Tada, *A Lifetime of Wisdom: Embracing the Way God Heals You* (Grand Rapids, MI: Zondervan, 2009).

Ravi K. Zacharias, *There Is a Plan* (Grand Rapids, MI: Zondervan, 2009).

Helpful Websites

Focus on the Family: www.family.org

National Center for Bullying Prevention: www.pacer.org/bullying/index.asp

DISCUSSION QUESTIONS

Question 1: What aspects often contribute to a person's self-image?

Question 2: Think of an area where you have been self-conscious. How did this make you feel?

Question 3: How has a negative view of how you were designed affected your behavior and relationships?

Question 4: What can you do to keep yourself from the destructive habit of making comparisons?

Question 5: Where does your attention go as you study a piece of art?

Question 6: Have you initially had trouble accepting a circumstance as God's design only to see later a bigger purpose than you could have imagined?

Question 7: How can we hold to absolute truths regarding sin and share our convictions without fostering bullying or instigating hate crimes?

Question 8: What additional confidence relating to self-image do people who have claimed Christ as Savior have?

SEARCHING FOR THE GREATER GOOD: THE STEM CELL DEBATE

Show me your ways, O LORD, teach me your paths; guide me in your truth.
PSALM 25:4-5

Life-Coach Leaders

We all face an uncertain future in this new world of biotechnology, which is moving forward at breakneck speed. We need great wisdom to grip this two-edged sword that presents so much promise not only for good but also for evil. When the Bible speaks of this modern era, it tells us that "many will go here and there to increase knowledge" (Dan. 12:4). In this session on stem cell research, you will help your small group discuss medical advances—the headlong race to increase knowledge—in light of God's Word. Participants will then be equipped to judge for themselves the best course of action. They'll be empowered to speak out with conviction in this strange new world of bioethics.

You and your group will be introduced to a lot of new terminology in this session. Don't let the words confuse you or your participants. Designer babies, cloning and growing new body parts sound like fascinating subjects, but there are two main points you will want to emphasize regarding the whole issue of stem cells. First, there is a marked difference between doing research using stem cells that come from embryos and stem cells that come from adult tissues. Second, this difference is highly debated because it raises questions about what it means to be a human person. This is where the secular worldview and the biblical worldview collide.

By the end of this session, you and your group may feel as if you've uncovered more questions than answers, and that's okay. For most people this is a challenging and unfamiliar topic. However, the next time participants hear a news report on stem cells, they'll understand not only what Scripture has to say about the subject but also why this issue is pivotal to the future of the human race.

What Are the Session Objectives?

In this session on the stem cell debate, participants will . . .

- Understand the different kinds of stem cell research
- Assess which research is producing successful medical therapies being used in modern treatments and cures
- Be equipped to explain some of the complexities of stem cell research to those who have questions

Why Should Participants Care?

The average American is deeply confused about the stem cell debate. A poll conducted by the Ethics and Public Policy Center revealed the public's lack of knowledge of the most basic facts about the question. While approximately 69 percent of those surveyed indicated that they were in favor of stem cell research, of that number, only 17 percent said they were familiar with the topic.[1]

A common criticism of people who oppose stem cell research is that they lack compassion for those whom the research could potentially benefit, such as people with spinal cord injuries, Parkinson's disease and Alzheimer's disease. To make matters worse, the media does more to muddy the water than to clarify the issue. For most people, the whole debate sounds rather abstract until some miraculous stem cell transplant is the only hope to save their life or the life of someone they love—then it becomes deeply personal!

Life in Real Time: Taking a Stand on Stem Cell Research

The Christian Institute on Disability at Joni and Friends produces policy papers reflecting our stand on issues that affect people with disabilities. We believe that all life is a gift from God and should be valued and respected. During President George W. Bush's eight years in office, there was a ban on using embryonic stem cells for research. Scientists were forced to focus on adult stem cells, and they had significant results. If this research can continue, the potential to cure diseases and injuries without destroying human embryos is amazing. Here is a portion of our policy paper on stem cell research:

Joni and Friends serves thousands of people with disabilities and their families. We believe it's unconscionable to tell these families to wait unnecessarily when—if more funding were available—even more cures would be available. "These adult stem cells—especially induced pluripotent stem cells—show more promise for cures than embryonic stem cells, and researchers are continuing to discover safer ways to inject them. Embryonic stem cell injections have led to the death of laboratory animals due to the formation of tumors, genetic instability and tissue rejection. And stem cells in the embryo can only be used by destroying it.

"For these reasons, we believe that embryonic stem cell research is not only flawed morally; it is flawed scientifically. It is a waste of time and money to conduct research on embryonic stem cells, and we cannot support President Obama's position in this matter."[2]

Laura Dominguez summed it up best in her testimony before the U.S. Senate Science Subcommittee when she said, "Scientists have been given the knowledge and tools to effectively use adult stem cell therapy, and they should take full advantage of that gift."[3] Policy papers on various topics, such as this one on stem cell research, are published by Joni and Friends. They are constantly updated to reflect current research and are available through the Christian Institute on Disability at www.joniandfriends.org/christian-institute-on-disability.

Leader Checklist

❑ Bibles

❑ Pens

❑ White Paper

❑ Copies of Session 5 discussion questions

❑ DVD keyed to session 5, "Searching for the Greater Good"

❑ News headlines on the stem cell debate

OVERVIEW

Welcome and Opening Prayer

Welcome participants and open in prayer, asking God to open their hearts and minds for understanding as you present issues during this session on the stem cell debate.

Opening Activity

Ask participants to break into groups of two or three. (Married couples should split up and join different groups.) Pass out a pen and single sheet of white paper to each person. Tell participants to tear out a paper doll and hold it up when they are finished. Then explain that they are to imagine that it is the year 2045, and each participant has decided to have a baby. With the tremendous advances in medical science that involve genetic selection, they have the option of designing the baby in advance. The paper doll is a prototype for the baby. Instruct the participants to write on the doll the kind of child they will request on their first visit to the World Center of Human Development and Bioethics. They can select gender, physical and mental characteristics, as well as the baby's potential areas of interest.

Allow three or four minutes for this activity, and then invite participants to introduce their baby to their small group. After this, gather all participants together and have two or three volunteers share their choices with the whole group. Then explain that we should shudder to think that technology could ever go so far as to put God's handiwork into human hands. However, scientists predict that while designer babies may be a couple of decades away, they will most definitely become a reality. It is one more step on the path to regenerative medicine.

Dr. Gregory Stock, Director of the Program on Medicine, Technology, and Society at UCLA's School of Public Health, shared his excitement about this emerging science during a debate in 2009 at Biola University in Southern California. He told the story of his meeting with a grieving couple whose 16-year-old son was dying. They loved him so much and would miss him so deeply that they wanted Dr. Stock's advice on cloning their son. Bioethicists like Dr. Stock believe that human cloning will one day be a humane and caring response to such hurting parents or to anyone who will be able to afford such technology. (Interested participants can watch several video clips on YouTube of Dr. Stock discussing his hopes for this ongoing research.)

Researchers are convinced that stem cells are the "Holy Grail" of medicine—that stem cells can provide cures for all sorts of medical conditions and can be manipulated to create a superior human race. Stem cells are the body's "master cells," meaning they are blank-slate cells that are very pliable and have the amazing ability to morph into almost any other kind of body tissue. For example, if you have a diseased liver or a bad heart, new tissues can be grown out of stem cells to replace your damaged ones. Who wouldn't want that? Give each member a copy of session 5 discussion questions (see page 97), and then ask the group the first discussion question.

Discussion Question #1

How difficult would it be for you to handle a medical diagnosis
of a disabling condition with an uncertain future?

Allow time for members to respond. Ask the group to consider how the psalmist and Jesus felt when facing difficult circumstances. Read Psalm 42:9-11 and Matthew 26:36-39.

Discussion Question #2

If you were told that your only hope for recovery from a devastating disease was
to have a stem cell transplant, what would be your initial reaction?

Ask group members to share one or two words to describe their possible reaction. Responses may include shock, fear, hope and/or confusion.

Introduction to "Searching for the Greater Good" on the *Life in the Balance* DVD

Explain that ever since Adam and Eve ate of the fruit in the garden, our lives have hung in the balance between good and evil. When Laura Dominguez was faced with permanent paralysis from a spinal cord injury, her family's determination to examine all possibilities for her recovery led them to one of the hottest topics of our times: stem cell research. While this advanced medical technology offers potential for good, it also poses some critical ethical questions.

Laura found strength in her faith in God, but she longed for something that could improve her abilities. She and her parents educated themselves on treatments for spinal cord injuries and stem cell transplants. They were desperate to get Laura back on her feet, but they could not play a part in destroying a human life. In this video, your group will witness the Dominguez family's journey (which ended up taking them all the way to Portugal) as they sought God's will for their daughter's future with grace and hope.

Your group will also learn how Christian professionals in bioethics and medicine are bringing a biblical perspective to the stem cell debate. These experts include Dr. Nigel Cameron, President of the Institution of Biotechnology and the Human Future; Dr. Richard Land, President of the Ethics and Religious Liberty Commission of the Southern Baptist Convention; and Dr. Kathy McReynolds, Director of the Public Policy Center at the Christian Institute on Disability at Joni and Friends.

Show the session 5 segment on the *Life in the Balance* DVD.

Life in the Word

Explain to the participants that as Christians, our biblical view of justice directs our attention to the weakest and most vulnerable in our midst. We are to recognize the equal worth of every person and should be ready to give our lives to relieve suffering. For that reason, we should wholeheartedly support stem cell research. Stem cells hold great promise. We want to draw attention to the many successes of stem cell transplants that have been used over the past two decades.

Discussion Question #3
*What are the two sources of stem cells? Can you recall from
the video any cures using adult stem cells?*

Allow time for members to respond. Answers to the second question may include juvenile diabetes, leukemia, lymphoma and/or other blood disorders. Share with the group that stem cells from adult tissues manufactured by the body are available from bone marrow, nasal tissue, dental pulp, certain fatty areas and blood. Umbilical cord blood has special properties to morph into other tissues.

Stem cells in human embryos in the earliest stages can potentially be programmed to grow into certain body tissues. But this potential has not been realized when it was tested on lab rats. Coupled with this fact is the way some researchers even refer to a human embryo—as a zygote or a blastocyst—terms that imply the embryo is not a human person. (Direct any participants interested in more information concerning the medical conditions that are currently being treated using adult stem cells to visit www.stemcellrearch.org.)

Have a volunteer read Genesis 1:27 and Jeremiah 1:5. Tell the group to keep the verses in mind as they consider their answer to discussion question #4.

Discussion Question #4

How sacred are human embryos? Should scientists be allowed to decide when life begins?

Allow time for group members to respond. Remind the group that Christians believe there is something exceptional—even sacred—about the human embryo that sets it apart; hundreds of thousands demonstrated this conviction by signing the Manhattan Declaration. And whether or not we believe that a soul inhabits a human embryo, though most Christians believe it does, the embryo is still not a goat, a chicken or a rat embryo. It is a human embryo. Each of us began our life journey as an embryo. No matter how infinitesimally small, a human embryo is owed all the moral and legal protection that any human life enjoys. As Dr. Kathy McReynolds, one of the experts seen on the video, stated, "What is clear from Scripture is that there is no such thing as a human non-person. Every single human being from the moment of conception is a human person who has fundamental rights to live."

Achieving Personal Balance

If your group members are not familiar with Jodi Picoult's book *My Sister's Keeper*, or the movie based on the book, explain that the story involves a child who was genetically engineered to be a perfect match for an older sister living with cancer. The parents loved all of their children and saw nothing wrong with Anna donating platelets, blood, her umbilical cord, and bone marrow to save her sister's life. Anna didn't have a problem with it either, but she decides to draw the line when she's asked to donate a kidney as a last-ditch attempt to save her sister's life. With her small savings in hand, Anna hires a lawyer to represent her in a medical emancipation suit to allow her to have control over her own body. The plot thickens as family, friends and community react to the unprecedented case. In the end, it's revealed that Anna's sick sister actually coerced Anna into protesting because she didn't want to undergo more medical procedures. Point out that while the story is tender and thought provoking, it doesn't address the core ethical issue of genetic engineering, which is what the parents used to create the perfect match for their sick daughter. What about the many human embryos that were destroyed before the parents found a perfect match to supply the necessary stem cells?

Discussion Question #5

Respond to this statement: Good and evil are not matters of opinion but are based on truth.

Ask a volunteer to read Genesis 2:9 and Genesis 3:22-24. In the creation story, God placed the tree of life—the tree of good and evil—in the middle of the Garden of Eden. A piece of fruit was plucked from the tree of the knowledge of good and evil, humankind's innocence was stripped away, and humans were left bearing the responsibility for knowledge—knowledge of what was good *and* evil. So the Lord God banished Adam and Eve from the Garden to work the ground from which Adam had been taken.

Share with the participants that some people think God was unkind in banishing Adam and Eve from the Garden. Some see the cherubim with the flaming sword as adding insult to injury. *Why would God make such a big deal about the tree of life?* Yet how merciful it was of God to keep sin-sick humans from eating of the tree of life! Had Adam and Eve been able to make their way back into the Garden, humankind would have lived forever in a sad and sorry state.

It's clear that knowledge, from the first time the word is used in the Bible, carries with it a sobering responsibility. It is a double-edged sword: Knowledge has a side that is good . . . and a side that is evil. It's been that way ever since the beginning. The tree of the knowledge of good and evil has a direct bearing on all that we've covered about stem cell research. With every medical advancement for good, there is always an accompanying potential for evil in terms of abuse—from splitting atoms to manipulating genes, from cloning to genetically designing an unborn child.

Discussion Question #6

*If scientists could clone you and use your cloned cells to cure your disease,
would you agree to the procedure? Why or why not?*

Allow time for group members to respond. Point out that by now, participants should understand that while this opportunity would be tempting, it opens a door to evil.

Balancing Faith and Culture

Pass out news headlines on the stem cell debate, and briefly discuss the opposing viewpoints presented by the headlines. Then ask discussion question #7.

Discussion Question #7

*As you consider competing opinions in modern society,
how has Jesus Christ been your moral compass?*

Allow time for members to share their thoughts. Responses will vary based on a person's Christian maturity and experiences. Read Psalm 41:1-2 and 1 Corinthians 6:19-20, and ask the participants to consider these verses as they answer discussion question 8.

Discussion Question #8

*How would you address the subject of embryonic stem cell research
with someone who is not a Christian?*

Point out that many people will find it practical to use all available medical technology to improve human life on planet earth. They may ask, "If an embryo will be destroyed anyway, why not use it for some good. If a prisoner will die for his crime, why not allow him to volunteer for life-threatening medical experiments." Ask the group if they can see how quickly this issue can escalate. Then go over with the group the differences between the biblical worldview and the scientific worldview of embryonic stem cell research. Tell the group what the biblical worldview is and ask the group to state what the contrasting scientific worldview is.

BIBLICAL WORLDVIEW	SCIENTIFIC WORLDVIEW
Serving God	Serving self
Improving human life	Creating human life
Repairing human life	Re-creating human life
Maintaining human life	Engineering human life
Cooperation with nature	Control over nature
Conformity to nature	Power over nature

Remind the group about what they learned about Laura Dominguez: Before her adult stem cell transplant, Laura could not feel her body, flex her wrists or stand using a walker. After the treatment, she had sensations in more of her body. With additional therapy, she recovered good movement in her upper body and minimal leg movement. These are miraculous steps for anyone with a spinal cord injury. Today, Laura trains 20 hours per week. She believes that nothing can threaten God's plan for her. She reads her Bible daily and prays for people with no hope. Her desire to help keep others from experiencing the depression she went through has led her to plan to open a gym for people with spinal cord injuries.

Closing Prayer

Praise God for the many people who have received life-giving adult stem cell transplants and as a result are healthier individuals.

Praise God for holding back the success of embryonic stem cell transplants and in so doing protecting the weakest among us.

Pray for wisdom and boldness to stand for biblical principles when opportunities arise.

Pray for funding to increase effective research in the use of adult stem cell transplants, and pray that new cures will be found to ease the pain of those who suffer.

Evaluating This Session

Were the session objectives met? Did participants come to understand that destroying one life in order to cure another is morally wrong? Do they feel equipped to discuss both sides of the ethical argument on stem cells? Were participants able to find answers in God's Word that allowed them to judge for themselves? Will they be better able to explore government initiatives that seek to expand funding for embryonic stem cell research?

Helpful Websites

The Center for Bioethics and Human Dignity: www.cbhd.org
The Family Research Council: www.frc.org
National Right to Life Committee: www.nrlc.org

DISCUSSION QUESTIONS

Question 1: How difficult would it be for you to handle a medical diagnosis of a disabling condition with an uncertain future?

Question 2: If you were told that your only hope for recovery from a devastating disease was to have a stem cell transplant, what would be your initial reaction?

Question 3: What are the two sources of stem cells? Can you recall from the video any cures using adult stem cells?

Question 4: How sacred are human embryos? Should scientists be allowed to decide when life begins?

Question 5: Respond to this statement: Good and evil are not matters of opinion but are based on truth.

Question 6: If scientists could clone you and use your cloned cells to cure your disease, would you agree to the procedure? Why or why not?

Question 7: As you consider competing opinions in modern society, how has Jesus Christ been your moral compass?

Question 8: How would you address the subject of embryonic stem cell research with someone who is not a Christian?

THE TRUTH BEHIND THE PAIN OF ABORTION

For you created my inmost being; you knit me together in my mother's womb. I praise you because I am fearfully and wonderfully made; your works are wonderful, I know that full well.

PSALM 139:13-14

Life-Coach Leaders

So many people have an automatic uneasiness about the issue of abortion. Their conscience tells them abortion is wrong, but they don't know how to articulate why it's wrong. Many are afraid to voice a pro-life opinion, because they know that their view will almost inevitably lead to an argument. It's not "fashionable" to oppose those who legitimize abortion as a "woman's right to choose." But shortly, equipped with the truth found in this chapter, participants will be prepared to intelligently discuss the subject and combat seemingly compassionate responses in support of abortion.

As a leader, you might find it tempting and quite easy to be snared by the thought that you have to change the minds of those participants who oppose the pro-life view. After all, you are telling them the truth. Rest assured that if you stick to the Word, God will be God and reveal how to deal with any opposition you may face. Make sure your only motive is to speak truth to each participant.

At the close of this session, encourage the participants to be self-assured and speak up now that they know the absolute truth. Remind them often of how truth sets people free (see John 8:32). Their words may be exactly what someone needs to be freed from a painful past involving abortion. People are searching for truth, but when it goes against their conscience, they tend to follow popular opinion, because it's the path of least resistance. When they learn the real truth, however, they often feel better about themselves and want to share it with those who have opposed them. Truth gives people the courage they otherwise lack.

As the leader, your task is to bridge the gaps between those dealing with the pain of abortion, those who are ambivalent regarding the subject and those who are adamant in their belief that abortion is either right or wrong. The goal is for all to meet on common ground in the end by applying God's Word (absolute truth) to the subject.

> *Courage is contagious. When a brave man takes a stand,*
> *the spines of others are often stiffened.*
> BILLY GRAHAM

What Are the Session Objectives?

In this session on abortion, participants will . . .

- Evaluate whether they have allowed the media or other outside sources to dictate their beliefs regarding abortion
- Recognize if their worldview truly comes from God's Word
- Direct those who are suffering after abortion on a clear path to spiritual and emotional healing
- Conclude that every life is a precious gift from God

Why Should Participants Care?

With more than 50 million abortions since 1973, abortion is bound to have affected each participant's life in one way or another.[1] Our country has placed its stamp of approval on abortions, and the result has been scores of people whose lives have been so affected that they've missed out on living up to their full potential. Men, women and children have been affected. When the numbers are divided among our population, an average of one out of every four women has chosen abortion. In the same light, one out of every four men has lost a child to abortion. Odds are good that you know someone who has had an abortion.

Too often, abortion is thought of as a way to solve a problem, but the evidence shows that for many women, the procedure brings further mental and physical complications that were not foreseen, including future miscarriages, infertility and ectopic pregnancies, and even breast cancer.[2] God's Word leaves no room for debate when it comes to life, and through the context of this session, each participant will realize the value God places on every human being. Our society has so little absolute truth that people are hungry for something they can stand on. This session on abortion is designed to give participants a strong foundation.

Ask God to minister to participants who have experienced an abortion in their past. Pray that they will find a new direction to healing. In an open dialogue based on God's Word, pray that they will take this opportunity to discuss their suffering.

Life in Real Time: The History of Abortion

Abortion existed years before it became legal in 1973. The topic became the controversial, divisive subject it is today after its legalization. Those who recognize abortion as a legal means of taking human life have fought tirelessly to reverse the law in our country. Those who believe each individual should have the right to choose abortion have fought just as hard. Because of the extreme actions on both sides (pro-choice and pro-life), many people avoid the subject entirely. Society prefers to leave this issue up to the government, and many believers and our churches have obliged.

As the leader of a small group studying this subject, remember that the conversation must focus on what Scripture says about abortion and life. Cling to the absolute truth and strive to leave opinions out of the discussion. If you have a divided group when it comes to abortion, God's Word will help keep unity (see Ps. 133:1).

As you approach this subject, do so with caution. Don't just jump right in and start lecturing on such a sensitive topic. Be responsive to the needs of the participants. Remember that if you have 10 people (men and women) in the group, probably 3 or 4 of them have had an abortion. Avoid words such as "murder" and "kill." Using harsh words can portray condemnation, which is not the purpose of this study.

Also be mindful of participants who are overzealous about the subject. Don't let this session turn into a political debate. Seeing abortion as a political issue is one way we have been taught to think, and it's wrong. Abortion may be dealt with politically at times, but it is not just a political issue. The taking of life is a subject God cares about deeply and wants Christians to take a stand against. As long as the politicians can keep this issue as their own, Christians can act as though it doesn't exist. Keep the focus on God's Word throughout this session.

Additional Scripture Reading on the Topic

In addition to the Scripture verses indicated throughout this session, here are a few more verses that you should read and that you may recommend to your group. First, regarding God's love toward life:

- **Genesis 9:6:** Killing a human being demonstrates contempt for God.
- **Jeremiah 1:5:** God knew us before we were placed in our mother's womb.
- **Matthew 5:21:** We are subject to judgment. We can't go against God's Word and not suffer consequences.

Regarding abortion in the cases of rape, incest or disability:

- **Exodus 4:11:** God is in control.
- **Deuteronomy 5:9-10:** God shows mercy to those who love Him and keep His commandments.
- **1 Samuel 2:6:** Life and death, prosperity and adversity should only be determined by the sovereign power of God.
- **Romans 9:20:** Who are we to ask God why or tell God that He made a mistake?

Keeping the Subject on Track

During the discussion periods, try to go around the room and allow each person to answer the questions. Try not to start with the same person each time. Start at different points in the room, and travel in opposite directions. This keeps any one person from dominating the class time. This practice will also encourage involvement from those who are quieter and keep them from hiding behind another person's eagerness to participate. You want *all* viewpoints to be heard and discussed so that people walk away knowing that they have thoroughly dissected this sensitive subject.

Leader Checklist

- ❑ Bibles
- ❑ Copies of session 6 discussion questions
- ❑ DVD keyed to session 6, "The Truth Behind the Pain of Abortion"
- ❑ News headlines on abortion

OVERVIEW

Welcome and Opening Prayer

Greet each participant and make him or her feel welcome. Open with prayer and give the group members time to settle and shake off the day.

Opening Activity

The purpose of the first discussion question is to get participants thinking and paying attention to the issue of abortion. In this section there is no right or wrong answer. The question is meant to simply break the ice and get focused. This is not the time for other group members to comment on another individual's answer.

Remember that abortion is a very divisive, controversial issue, so insist on unity and respect for others. Give each member a copy of the session 6 discussion questions (see page 111), and then read Psalm 133:1. In light of this verse, ask the group the first discussion question.

Discussion Question #1

How do you feel when the subject of abortion is brought up in conversation?

Ask group members to share one-word responses, and then pass out news headlines on abortion and briefly discuss any bias evident in each headline. Following this, invite participants to answer the second discussion question to give you insight into each group member's worldview.

Discussion Question #2

What or who helped you develop your belief system regarding the issue of abortion?

Introduction to "The Truth Behind the Pain of Abortion" on the *Life in the Balance* DVD

In this session's video segment, your group will meet the all-American Guthrie family. After a normal pregnancy with their son, the Guthries welcomed their first daughter, Hope.

But shortly after the birth, these parents discovered that their daughter had a deadly genetic disease named Zellweger syndrome. Infants with it have a life expectancy of only 6 to 12 months.

The parents, David and Nancy Guthrie, accepted their daughter's certain death and chose not to blame God or let bitterness set in. Instead, they submitted to whatever God wanted for them. We can all learn from their words:

Nancy: Here [this situation] was going to prove if I really believed what I said I believed my entire life.

David: We chose to trust God.

Nancy: We didn't want to fight against God's will but rather submit to it.

David: We knew Hope was a gift from God, a life placed in our care.

When Nancy was surprised to find herself pregnant again, the Guthries discovered that the just-forming child would also be born with the rare syndrome. When the doctor asked the couple to come to his office to discuss their options, the Guthries informed him that abortion was not an option. Although the anguish of saying goodbye to Hope was still a painful memory, they also remembered the great joy her short life had brought to them. They were willing to go through the same pain with their son Gabriel, because it meant being able to experience the unspeakable joy God gives through each precious life.

Participants will learn from the Guthries' heart-wrenching story that submission to a sovereign God holds all aspects of life together. The Guthries' choice to trust God with their suffering put their situation into a whole new context. They could no longer look at life the same way they had before. They attest to becoming better people for having known Hope and Gabriel and for caring for them with dignity and respect. Show the session 6 segment on the *Life in the Balance* DVD. (Be aware that as your group watches this video, raw emotion from some participants may be evoked. Some participants will reflect on past choices in regard to life and realize they've made mistakes.)

Life in the Word

Read Psalm 139:13-16. Ask a volunteer to read aloud verse 14 again. Then ask the third discussion question.

Discussion Question #3

How does verse 14 of Psalm 139 describe how each life is made?

The answer should be "fearfully and wonderfully."

Discussion Question #4

What does "fearfully and wonderfully" mean to you?

Allow time for members to respond. Answers will vary but may include created, designed, planned and/or divinely orchestrated.

Explain to the group that because God made us as eternal beings, we will one day stand before Him to be judged as wicked or righteous. Just because a child may be conceived by a wicked parent doesn't mean that he or she is condemned to do evil. God starts each life off with a clean slate, fearfully and wonderfully.

Read 1 Samuel 2:6 and Ezekiel 18:20. Tell the group that these verses make it clear that only in the authority of our sovereign God is there power to choose life or death. He is the only One who should make these decisions, not us. When we take on this mantle, it is too heavy for us. We are bound to fail under the pressure. These choices are for the Creator to make.

Achieving Personal Balance

Tell the participants that the word "absolute" can be defined as free from imperfection, complete, perfect, pure, not limited in any way, ultimate, positive or certain. The way to find balance is by applying absolute truth: truth found in God's Word. Scripture is not limited by our society or situational ethics. It's truth we can rely on in any situation.

Discussion Question #5

What is one belief you have held to but now question because of what you learned in this session?

Allow time for members to respond. At this point, the group members who have a worldview that doesn't line up with Scripture may start to question their view.

Share with the group the following words from one individual whose worldview changed to align with the biblical worldview: "I always believed abortion was wrong, but didn't feel right about trying to make others believe that way. I don't like prostitution and drug use either, and I'm thankful for laws against that. Now I believe there should be laws against this too, because now I see that abortion really is ending another human life."

Discussion Question #6

What is the "absolute truth" you can apply to that belief?

Allow time for members to respond. Share the following example: "When I heard David Guthrie say, 'This was a life entrusted to our care,' it really made me see that God gives life

107

and it's precious, and we should care for it regardless of our convenience, or whether or not that life was planned by us. It was planned by God and that's all that matters."

Have participants form two groups. Assign one group the secular worldview and the other the biblical worldview. Have each group work together as a team. Ask the secular worldview group to tell a common perspective on abortion, and then ask the biblical worldview group to respond with an absolute truth based on Scripture. Do this as long as time allows and try to make sure that the major arguments for abortion are covered. This exercise will help participants learn the different arguments and how to combat them with biblical truth.

Balancing Faith and Culture

Read Genesis 1:27. Point out to the group that when we have children, they are created in our image, and we love them very much. If someone hurts our child, we regard that hurt as a serious, personal offense. God creates every life in His image and His love for each life is immeasurable. When that life is destroyed, a wound deep in God's soul is created, just as when a mother or father loses a child. We must protect God's children, just as we would protect our own.

Discussion Question #7
Tell why you do or why you don't believe the following quote from the Manhattan Declaration to be true: "A culture of death inevitably cheapens life in all its stages and conditions by promoting the belief that lives that are imperfect, immature or inconvenient are discardable."

Allow time for the group to give their personal responses to the question. Remind the group that when people sit silently, that silence implies compliance. We cannot remain silent regarding this culture of death our society has bought into. There is too much at stake for implied compliance.

Read Romans 12:2. Note for the group that by studying what the Word of God has to say regarding abortion, they are renewing their minds toward the things of God. They will no longer allow this world to force them to conform to its view; rather, they will be enabled to find and prove the good and perfect will of God.

Read John 10:10. Point out to the participants that when a culture steals futures, brings death to infants and destroys lives, there is only one culprit: the thief. (If any participant is in doubt about exactly who this thief is, tell the group that it is Satan.)

Discussion Question #8

How can John 10:10 be used as a "dividing line" in the Bible?

Allow volunteers to share their opinions, and then emphasize to the group that whatever is stealing, bringing death or destroying comes from Satan. Whatever is giving life comes from God through the sacrifice of His Son, Jesus Christ. When we have a choice to make regarding life, all we have to do is filter that decision through this verse. Then we'll know that if our answer gives life, it is from God; if it takes life, it is from Satan.

Before the session ends, take a few moments to address those who have had an abortion, if they have spoken to the group about it. If no one has spoken up but you have an idea who has had an abortion, do not single anyone out. Simply assure participants that if they know someone who is suffering mentally, emotionally or spiritually from a past abortion, you would be glad to direct them to an organization dedicated to helping men and women understand God's forgiveness and healing after an abortion. You may even want to print out a recommended list of resources and/or websites, and post the list somewhere in the room.

Closing Prayer

As you close this session, take a moment to reflect through prayer on all God has provided and shown the group. Thank Him for His provision and for His truth that sets people free.

Pray that the women who have had an abortion (and the men affected by abortion) will be set free from any negative effects, so they can go forward and tell others about the life-saving truth.

Take time to pray for the week ahead and for the momentum and excitement that is building, and pray that all of the information will be deeply embedded in the hearts and minds of everyone present.

Evaluating the Session

Were the session objectives met? Did each participant come to realize whether he or she had allowed media and outside sources to influence their beliefs regarding abortion? Did the group members change your view on abortion or teach you something significant? If so, what? Thinking of the comments shared during this week's discussions, are there any participants who might have a hard time with next week's subject? If so, what is a specific prayer you can pray for that person?

Recommended Resources

Sheila Harper, *SaveOne: A Guide to Emotional Healing After Abortion* (North Little Rock, AR: SaveOne, 2003).

Shiela Harper, *SaveOne: The Men's Study* (North Little Rock, AR: SaveOne, 2003).

Nancy Guthrie, *Holding On to Hope: A Pathway Through Suffering to the Heart of God* (Wheaton, IL: Tyndale, 2002).

Helpful Websites

SaveOne: http://www.saveone.org

Zellweger Syndrome: http://www.zellwegersyndrome.org

Nancy Guthrie: http://www.nancyguthrie.com

Pregnancy Resource Centers: http://www.cpclink.com

DISCUSSION QUESTIONS

Question 1: How do you feel when the subject of abortion is brought up in conversation?

Question 2: What or who helped you develop your belief system regarding the issue of abortion?

Question 3: How does verse 14 of Psalm 139 describe how each life is made?

Question 4: What does "fearfully and wonderfully" mean to you?

Question 5: What is one belief you have held to but now question because of what you learned in this session?

Question 6: What is the "absolute truth" you can apply to that belief?

Question 7: Tell why you do or why you don't believe the following quote from the Manhattan Declaration to be true: "A culture of death inevitably cheapens life in all its stages and conditions by promoting the belief that lives that are imperfect, immature or inconvenient are discardable."

Question 8: How can John 10:10 be used as a "dividing line" in the Bible?

A CALLOUSED CONSCIENCE: EUGENICS AND GENOCIDE

Speak up for those who cannot speak for themselves,
for the rights of all who are destitute.

Proverbs 31:8

THEY CAME FIRST for the Communists,
and I didn't speak up because I wasn't a Communist.
THEN THEY CAME for the Jews,
and I didn't speak up because I wasn't a Jew.
THEN THEY CAME for the trade unionists,
and I didn't speak up because I wasn't a trade unionist.
THEN THEY CAME for the Catholics,
and I didn't speak up because I was a Protestant.
THEN THEY CAME for me
and by that time no one was left to speak up.
PASTOR MARTIN NIEMÖLLER[1]

Life-Coach Leaders

We study the attempted extermination of the Jewish people by the Nazi regime during World War II, and we shake our heads. We cringe as we watch the historical drama *Hotel Rwanda*, documenting the annihilation of 800,000 Rwandans in 1994, at the hands of their own countrymen. How could this happen? What kind of people could do such a thing? History has proven that almost anyone can fall prey to the prejudice, ignorance and self-preservation that precede genocide. You might even be an unwitting participant, going along for all the "right" reasons.

What Are the Session Objectives?

In this session on eugenics and genocide, participants will . . .

- Understand the history of the eugenics movement in the United States and Europe
- Grasp how a biblical worldview has no room for social engineering
- Learn how to advocate on behalf of those who are endangered by the eugenics movement

Why Should Participants Care?

In Proverbs 31:8 we're told to "speak up for those who cannot speak for themselves, for the rights of all who are destitute." Unborn children cannot speak from the womb. Yet statistics tell us that when Down syndrome is diagnosed prenatally, 84 to 91 percent of those babies are aborted.[2] Although participants in the study may not have a direct connection to someone with Down syndrome, Christians are called to stand up for what is right. We must understand that when we toy with social engineering or eliminate a life that society deems unworthy, we are ultimately questioning God's sovereignty. And when we tolerate policies aimed at the most vulnerable, we also allow the government to usurp God's authority over the very lives He commanded us to protect.

Life in Real Time: Learning About Eugenics/Genocide

Genocide is not just something that happened in the past or in uncivilized nations; it's happening here and now. In 1948, the United Nations Convention on the Prevention and Punishment of the Crime of Genocide defined genocide as any of the following acts committed with *intent to destroy, in whole or in part,* a national, ethnical, racial or religious group, as such:

- Killing members of the group
- Causing serious bodily or mental harm to members of the group
- Deliberately inflicting on the group conditions of life calculated to bring about its physical destruction in whole or in part
- *Imposing measures intended to prevent births within the group*
- Forcibly transferring children of the group to another group[3]

When the American College of Obstetricians and Gynecologists began recommending broader prenatal testing for Down syndrome, starting in 2007, they did not view their recommendation as leading to genocide. But the facts speak for themselves: Fewer people with Down syndrome are being born today because of the recommendation to routinely test *all* mothers-to-be, not just those with high-risk pregnancies, so more abortions are being performed.

In the video segment for today's session, "A Calloused Conscience," participants will meet 53-year-old Robin Hiser and hear how her life has impacted those around her. Although Robin and her young nephew both have Down syndrome, participants will see how much they enjoy life and all it has to offer, despite their disability. Members will also hear from Sib Charles, Pennsylvania Program Director at Joni and Friends, who has witnessed the decline in the number of people born with Down syndrome. She says on the DVD segment:

> I see that it's genocide. That we are trying to obliterate a whole population of Down's people because they aren't perfect. We are wiping out a population, but we don't want to call it that because it's not politically correct, or it's too strong of a word. But that's what's going to happen.

While the term "genocide" produces images of death and devastation in people, many participants may not be familiar with the term "eugenics." Those participants who have heard the word may automatically associate Hitler and World War II with it because of its close association with Nazi abuses, such as human experimentation and the extermination of "undesired" population groups.

If the members of your group are not clear about what eugenics is, tell them that it is selective breeding applied to human beings in order to improve the species. Back in the middle of the nineteenth century, Francis Galton theorized that a better society would be created if superior men and women were to marry each other and produce "more fit" children. It was Galton who coined the famous word "eugenics," which literally means "good genes." Without the negative associations, it may sound like another miracle of science. After all, the idea of ridding the human race of defective genes sounds quite noble. Who wouldn't choose to have good genes or healthier DNA? The problem is that other human beings would be sacrificed for "the greater good." We as Christians, however, believe that every person is created in the image of God, and therefore no person is less valuable than another (see Ps. 139:13-16).

Leader Checklist

- ❑ Bible
- ❑ One paper clip for each participant and a small clear container filled with paper clips (that have been counted)
- ❑ Copies of session 7 discussion questions
- ❑ News headlines on Down syndrome, genocide and/or genetic engineering
- ❑ DVD keyed to session 7, "A Calloused Conscience"
- ❑ Optional: Viewing screen and Internet access

OVERVIEW

Welcome and Opening Prayer

Welcome participants and open the session with prayer, asking God to open their hearts and minds for understanding as you discuss these issues about eugenics and genocide.

Opening Activity

Help cement the key concepts of genocide, solidarity with those facing persecution, and how small efforts can have a big impact by passing out a single paper clip to each of the participants and sharing this story with your group:

In 1998, middle school students from the small Tennessee town of Whitwell were learning about the Holocaust. They struggled to grasp the enormity of the devastation—an estimated 6,000,000 Jews were killed between 1939 and 1945. They came up with an idea to collect 6,000,000 paper clips representing the lives lost. The students chose the paper clip after learning that it had become a symbol of resistance to the German invasion of Norway. Since Norwegians were banned from wearing flag pins or any other patriotic symbols, the paper clip on a lapel took on a new meaning of solidarity and unity, being bound together in resistance.

The students wrote letters to friends, family and even celebrities to increase awareness of the Paper Clip Project and ask for paper clip donations. After garnering media attention, the small project evolved into one gaining worldwide support, and donations from thousands, including presidents and celebrities.

Many of the paper clips were accompanied by letters from survivors, and other Holocaust memorabilia. The students, staff and the community of Whitwell opened the Children's Holocaust Memorial in 2001 to display the paper clips and other priceless memorabilia collected. The most substantial donation was an actual train car used to transport victims to concentration, labor, and death camps during World

War II. The German rail car now sits on display, housing 11 million paper clips. At last count, over 30 million paper clips had been received.[4]

Tell the group that the Paper Clip Project was so inspiring that in 2004 a documentary film was released, telling the story of how a lesson about prejudice became a story of hope and inspiration.[5]

Now point to the container filled with paper clips. Tell the group the following:

There are _____ paper clips in this container. Try to think about each clip as representing a person.

I'd like for each of you to wear your paper clip as a reminder of what's at stake—real lives. You may or may not be familiar with Jewish customs, but in Scripture we see how God instituted many of their traditions, even their clothing, to remind them of who they were, to whom they belonged, and what He expected of them. According to Numbers 15:38-40, God told Moses to instruct the Israelites to sew tassels on the ends of their garments, so that they "will remember to obey all my commands and will be consecrated to your God" (v. 40).

Give each member a copy of the session 7 discussion questions (see page 125), and then ask the group the first discussion question.

Discussion Question #1
How do you think you would have fared under Hitler's regime?

Allow time for several members to share. Explain to the group that the "survival of the fittest" mindset during World War II went so far as to eliminate those with the wrong hair or eye color, according to Hitler's standards. Some of the first people disposed of were those with disabilities who had no families or no one to stand up for them. The Nazi regime called this their Euthanasia Program, but that was merely a euphemism. The program's chief aim was to cleanse society of people considered genetically defective and a burden to society.[6] Although eugenics was one of the dominant movements in America in the first part of the century, once Nazi Germany adopted eugenics, they took it to its logical conclusion—the complete annihilation of *anyone* considered defective: Jews, Gypsies, the elderly, the mentally impaired and people with physical disabilities.

Point out that our nation desperately needs advocates for the weak. The Nazi medical teams looked for disabled people who had no friends, no family members, no advocates or visitors. They selected only people who had no one to speak up for them.[7] Help your group see how important it is to be a voice for the weak—to speak up for those who are too small or too old to speak up for themselves, to voice a clear biblical worldview that upholds the sacredness of all life, and to stand in opposition to those who would seek to diminish or even do away with anyone considered "too defective."

Read Psalm 82:3-4 and Isaiah 61, and then ask discussion question #2.

Discussion Question #2

How do you believe our society views weakness compared to how God views weakness?

Allow time for a few members to respond. Pass out news headlines on Down syndrome, genocide and/or genetic engineering and allow participants to relate what the headlines reflect about societal views of the subject. Explain that we don't like weakness in ourselves, or in society overall. We love slogans like "Power to the people!" and "Just do it!" We relish stories of people who are "self-made" and have "pulled themselves up by their bootstraps." The Bible, however, paints a much different picture of weakness. The image of God is *especially* mirrored in the weak; that is, the medically fragile, the elderly and people with profound disabilities. God intentionally brings brokenness and weakness to those He loves. In fact, many times those who God wants to use most are broken for His sovereign purposes. And broken, weak people display the image of God most convincingly when they lean on Him for strength moment by moment. God's image is made most glorious when He is shown to be the one and only sustainer of those who are weak.

Read and reflect on Genesis 32:24-32, which describes how Jacob wrestled with the man of God, who wrenched Jacob's hip out of its socket. Jacob became disabled, for the verse says that "he was limping because of his hip" (v. 31). When God met Jacob and left him wounded, that physical wound was meant to remind Jacob of his spiritual brokenness. He could no longer feign moral strength as he limped through life with his new physical disability. Dan Allender, in his book *Leading with a Limp,* says, "[Jacob's] limp is a reminder that when God renames us, He also makes each one of us a new person through a redemption that requires brokenness."[8]

Read 1 Corinthians 1:27-30 and 2 Corinthians 4:7, and tell the group to keep these verses in mind as they watch the video.

Introduction to "A Calloused Conscience" on the *Life in the Balance* DVD

In today's video segment, your group will meet Robin Hiser and many of her family members. Robin has been an active volunteer at Joni and Friends Family Retreats for many years.

She loves our Lord, and her worship is something to be admired. We've mentioned how the eugenics movement is trying to rid society of "undesirables." In this video your group will meet a joyful, engaging, caring person whose relationship with the Lord is something we should all desire to emulate. Your group is sure to be moved as Robin shares her struggles against prejudice and preconceived notions and gives you a glimpse into her life as a person living with Down syndrome. Show the session 7 segment on the *Life in the Balance* DVD.

Life in the Word

Begin this section by asking the participants the third discussion question.

Discussion Question #3
*Did Robin and her nephew, Collin, dispel any preconceived notions
you had about people with Down syndrome?*

Allow volunteers to answer, and then explain that the impetus for social engineering, or eugenics, is to produce healthy, attractive, gifted children in order to have more productive and happier adults. The problem with this idea lies in the fact that healthy, attractive and gifted adults are, in fact, no more likely to be happy than disabled, unattractive or unintelligent people.

Point out to the group that Robin is one of the happiest people you could ever meet. In fact, it's well known that Down syndrome produces people who are generally happier than the rest of us! Although Robin has a genetic abnormality, she serves on the leadership team every summer for the Joni and Friends Family Retreat in Pennsylvania. She has a passion for Jesus Christ and a deep desire to give the love of her Savior to others. Robin doesn't understand how to keep up with the Joneses or how to get over her head in debt, but she does know how to unreservedly share her love for Christ with everyone she meets. While Robin never married, men and women with Down syndrome do marry, and the relationships thus formed are honest-to-goodness models to neighbors and friends.

Read Habakkuk 3:17-19 and 1 Thessalonians 5:16-18. Emphasize to the participants that each person, no matter his or her circumstances, should be joyful and praise God, much like Robin does.

Discussion Question #4
What did Robin mean when she called her mother a hero?

Allow time for group members to respond. Ideas should include the fact that it is a brave thing to welcome a child with disabilities into a family and that it takes courage to help a child with disabilities succeed right alongside other siblings.

Relate to your group the following story:

Baby Doe, a boy, was born in 1982 with Down syndrome and an obstruction in the food pipe, which could have been resolved by a simple, routine operation. Almost any surgeon within a 50-mile radius of the hospital could have performed the procedure, but his parents refused. Instead, they decided to allow their child to starve to death. When word of the situation became public, a dozen families came forward and offered to adopt the baby, but the parents said no. Though it would have cost them no money, time or effort to allow someone else to raise their child, the parents, their doctors and the Supreme Court of Indiana said the parents had the right to starve the child to death. Seven days after his birth, Baby Doe died in a back room of the hospital. The U.S. Supreme Court never had time to hear the appeal.

Allow a few moments of silence for this story to sink in. (As an option, you can also show the powerful and stirring YouTube video "Baby Doe" by Steve Taylor.[9])

Achieving Balance in Life

Point out to the group that many people would argue that Baby Doe was better off dead because his quality of life would have been extremely low. Not only do we see this myth dispelled in the vibrant life of Robin Hiser, but also as Christians we have to ask, "Who is the judge?" Have a volunteer read Ecclesiastes 11:5, and then ask discussion question #5.

Discussion Question #5
What gives life value?

Allow time for members to respond. Explain that too often in our society, people are treated as *things*, not human beings with intrinsic value. We "have" no value because society no longer believes we are created, or made in the image of God. Instead, our humanity is shaped by subjective (not objective) values, such as one's comfort or another's convenience, or an ability to function or relate meaningfully to others. These values give shape to the *quality-of-life* ethic. Such an ethic extols the strong and minimizes the life value of the weak or fragile.

God made us, both weak and strong, in His image. Humankind reflects Him in a way other created beings do not. Read Psalm 72:4,12-14. Help your group understand that God promotes the sacredness of every individual, and He defeats those who try to abort and euthanize human beings. Ask the group members to listen carefully as you read aloud the following excerpt from the Manhattan Declaration:

A culture of death inevitably cheapens life in all its stages and conditions by promoting the belief that lives that are imperfect, immature or inconvenient are discardable. As predicted by many prescient persons, the cheapening of life that began with abortion has now metastasized. For example, human embryo-destructive research and its public funding are promoted in the name of science and in the cause of developing treatments and cures for diseases and injuries. The President and many in Congress favor the expansion of embryo-research to include the taxpayer funding of so-called "therapeutic cloning." This would result in the industrial mass production of human embryos to be killed for the purpose of producing genetically customized stem cell lines and tissues. At the other end of life, an increasingly powerful movement to promote assisted suicide and "voluntary" euthanasia threatens the lives of vulnerable elderly and disabled persons. Eugenic notions such as the doctrine of lebensunwertes Leben ("life unworthy of life") were first advanced in the 1920s by intellectuals in the elite salons of America and Europe. Long buried in ignominy after the horrors of the mid-20th century, they have returned from the grave. The only difference is that now the doctrines of the eugenicists are dressed up in the language of "liberty," "autonomy," and "choice." . . .

Our concern is not confined to our own nation. Around the globe, we are witnessing cases of genocide and "ethnic cleansing," the failure to assist those who are suffering as innocent victims of war, the neglect and abuse of children, the exploitation of vulnerable laborers, the sexual trafficking of girls and young women, the abandonment of the aged, racial oppression and discrimination, the persecution of believers of all faiths, and the failure to take steps necessary to halt the spread of preventable diseases like AIDS. We see these travesties as flowing from the same loss of the sense of the dignity of the human person and the sanctity of human life that drives the abortion industry and the movements for assisted suicide, euthanasia, and human cloning for biomedical research. And so ours is, as it must be, a truly consistent ethic of love and life for all humans in all circumstances.

Discussion Question #6

How would you summarize what the Manhattan Declaration says about life?

Allow a few volunteers to respond before continuing on to the next section.

Balancing Faith and Culture

Review the following chart with participants to compare the secular worldview, which can exploit God's design, and the biblical worldview, which honors God's design.

SECULAR WORLDVIEW	BIBLICAL WORLDVIEW
Survival of the fittest	When I'm weak, then I'm strong
Subjective quality of life	Created in the image of God
Power, beauty, success, riches	Godliness with contentment
Look out for number one	Love others more than self

Help members see that the secular worldview contains the seeds of the crop that have harvested the destruction of millions of people throughout human history.

Discussion Question #7
Now that your eyes have been opened to genocide and eugenics in both the past and present, what do you think about such manipulations?

Allow time for members to respond. Explain that because we live in a fallen world and have a distorted human nature, even Christians tend to extol the bright and beautiful, the gifted and the strong. Our natural reaction is to side with attractive leader types and ignore those we feel would drain our energies or require too much of us. We have a tendency to exclude the weak or unlovely, but the truth is that we need each other. First Corinthians 12:22-24 says, "On the contrary, those parts of the body that seem to be weaker are indispensable, and the parts that we think are less honorable we treat with special honor. And the parts that are unpresentable are treated with special modesty, while our presentable parts need no special treatment." Note to the participants that the Bible states, "those parts . . . that *seem* to be weaker" and "the parts that we *think* are less honorable." From the world's point of view, people who are infirm *are* weak and *have no* honor—that's the impetus behind the eugenics movement. But from God's point of view, these people are strong as they lean on Him, and they have honor because they understand the source of their help (see 2 Cor. 12:10 and Jas. 1:9).

Read 2 Corinthians 12:9 and 1 Timothy 2:1-2. Explain to the group that they must be prepared for God to use them. They are called to be prayer warriors to intercede on behalf of the weak and vulnerable, as well as for those in authority to honor God in their decisions. The group also needs to remember Robin Hiser and Baby Doe, especially when someone

123

asks for their advice or input. Finally, remind the group to use whatever power and influence they've been given to change policies and reveal hidden agendas.

Closing Prayer

As you conclude, ask participants if they have any prayer requests to share with the group. Please remind them about their paper clips and the fact that each one symbolizes a life.

Pray for our nation, our leadership and every person created in the image of God.

Pray for our hearts to be softened to those who need us most, and ask for forgiveness for all of the times we turned away from their needs.

Pray for this lesson to bear much fruit in the lives of the participants.

Evaluating the Session

Were the session objectives met? Did the discussion questions address the issues raised by participants? Were the participants equipped to go forward as instructed? Was there anyone who might need follow-up or seemed particularly moved by the topic?

Recommended Resources

Stephanie O. Hubach, *Same Lake, Different Boat: Coming Alongside People Touched by Disability* (Phillipsburg, NJ: P&R Publishing, 2006).

Dan Allender, *Leading with a Limp: Take Full Advantage of Your Most Powerful Weakness* (Colorado Springs, CO: Waterbrook Press, 2008).

Helpful Websites

American Life League: www.all.org

American Bioethics Advisory Commission: www.all.org/abac/

National Down Syndrome Society: http://www.ndss.org/

DISCUSSION QUESTIONS

Question 1: How do you think you would have fared under Hitler's regime?

Question 2: How do you believe our society views weakness compared to how God views weakness?

Question 3: Did Robin and her nephew, Collin, dispel any preconceived notions you had about people with Down syndrome?

Question 4: What did Robin mean when she called her mother a hero?

Question 5: What gives life value?

Question 6: How would you summarize what the Manhattan Declaration says about life?

Question 7: Now that your eyes have been opened to genocide and eugenics in both the past and present, what do you think about such manipulations?

FROM OBSCURITY TO CELEBRITY BY WAY OF TRAGEDY: END-OF-LIFE ISSUES

The path of the godly leads to life. So why fear death?
PROVERBS 12:28, *TLB*

Life-Coach Leaders

Many people will remember the media circus that surrounded the life and death of Terri Schiavo. Participants may have discussed her case with co-workers, neighbors or prayer groups. The controversy drew protesters on both sides of the issue, as had similar cases like Karen Quinlan's in 1976 and Nancy Cruzan's in 1990. In each situation there was a question over whether the patient would want to be kept alive through medical interventions. Since none of the patients had left their wishes in writing with their signatures, family members were forced into court to speak on the behalf of each patient. However, in the Schiavo case, family members could not agree, and the case went all the way to the U.S. Supreme Court.

Before you begin this session, put a tissue in one of your pockets and a rock in another pocket. This will remind you to tread gently into this weighty subject. Be prepared to help participants with hard opinions lay down their own "rocks," and be ready to use a tissue to wipe away the tears of those whose hearts are tender on these end-of-life issues.

What Are the Session Objectives?

In this session on end-of-life issues, participants will . . .

- Examine the implications of Terri Schiavo's story on our society as a whole as well as on individual families
- Understand the importance of having a health care directive
- Understand what the Bible says about life worth living and human dignity
- Become equipped to provide moral guidance to a family like Terri Schiavo's

Why Should Participants Care?

We are well aware of the fact that we will all die someday, but it's not a topic we like to discuss—not even with family members. The Schiavo family found themselves in a battle because Terri didn't have a health care directive that spelled out her wishes for her life. While doctors and lawyers had hoped that her case would drive people to be more prepared, it did little to increase the estimated 20 to 30 percent of the people in the U.S. who have a signed health care proxy or advance medical directive.

Such documents (known by different names in different states) pertain to a patient's treatment preferences and designate a surrogate decision maker in the event that the person becomes unable to make his or her own medical decisions. If participants have served as a surrogate for someone in the past, invite them to give a brief account of their experiences. However, avoid long family stories, which can potentially dominate a session on this topic.

Because there are two parts to the video segment for this session, it would be ideal if you would be able to spend two weeks on this subject, as you could show each 30-minute part. However, if your time is limited, preview the videos with your small group in mind and select various portions that you wish to emphasize in your teaching session.

Life in Real Time: End-of-Life Issues

Hospice care is believed to have started as far back as the eleventh century when care was given to terminally ill patients. However, it wasn't widespread until the 1700s, when the

Catholic Church began to establish the Sisters of Charity in France.[1] The word "hospice" means serving double-duty and includes a philosophy of hospitable, end-of-life care for people in hospitals or in their own homes. Perhaps you know of a hospice caregiver or have considered becoming one. If so, consider the following case study used to help new trainees know what to expect of a patient.

The patient is unable to feed himself and must be spoon-fed; constant monitoring is required due to the dangers of choking. Food is often regurgitated. The patient babbles incoherently and is generally non-communicative, combative and uncooperative when given instructions. He is often frustrated and can become violently angry when not given his way. Sleep patterns are erratic. The patient is incontinent, having no control over his bowel and bladder functions. What would your response be to the prospect of caring for such a person? Disgust? Dread? Repulsion? Many of us would probably insist that we couldn't watch constant indignities. We couldn't endure such sad, ongoing demands with little reprieve or appreciation.

But what if you discovered that the individual being described above was a healthy, bouncing, four-month-old baby boy? That would present an entirely different picture, wouldn't it? But why should it? Aren't caring for a precious newborn and caring for a fellow human bring who is dying the same gift of God? Are not the feet of those who run to rock the cradle as beautiful as the feet of those who run to the side of a hospice patient's bed? If we are to emulate the Great Physician who pulled little children onto His lap and also caressed the hands of lepers, then, beloved, we *can do this!*

Leader Checklist

- ❑ Bibles
- ❑ Family album with black-and-white photos of ancestors
- ❑ News headlines on end-of-life issues, Karen Quinlan, Nancy Cruzan and/or Terri Schiavo
- ❑ Copies of Session 8 Discussion Questions
- ❑ DVD keyed to part 1 of "The Terri Schiavo Story"
- ❑ Paper and pens

OVERVIEW

Welcome and Opening Prayer

Welcome participants and open in prayer asking God to open their hearts and minds for understanding as you discuss with them these difficult end-of-life issues.

Opening Activity

Show some of the pages of the family album with black-and-white photos of ancestors. Encourage participants to share a few memories of stories about their ancestors. As participants look through the album, tell them that life and death must have been simpler in our great-grandparent's day. People died younger in life. Some died of epidemics like the black plague or cholera, others in coalmines, still others during childbirth, and many in war. They died without being attached to beeping machines, respirators or feeding tubes. Their loved ones may have argued over who would get the family farm but not over removing their life-support devices. And people respected the dead in the same way they would have wanted to be respected at their own passing. Death with dignity was the expected rule. And some cowboys were buried with their boots on!

Today's medical technologies allow us to live longer and healthier lives. We are grateful for trained medical teams that fill trauma centers with the latest lifesaving devices. Incredible surgical procedures restore human organs and lead to cures for diseases. We can get relief from much of our suffering and pain. In the worst of conditions, we can be kept alive through extraordinary measures. But when our time to die comes, we can face a whole menu of options.

Pass out the news headlines on end-of-life issues, Karen Quinlan, Nancy Cruzan and/or Terry Schiavo, and briefly discuss any bias shown by the wording in each headline. Give each member a copy of the session 8 discussion questions (see page 139), and then ask the group the first discussion question.

Discussion Question #1

*Why do you think that stories like Karen Quinlan's, Nancy Cruzan's
and Terri Schiavo's captured such national attention?*

Allow time for group members to share their thoughts. Responses may include their youth, conflicting medical opinions, grieving family, and/or if it could happen to them it could happen to anyone.

Introduction to "The Terri Schiavo Story" on the *Life in the Balance* DVD

Explain to the group that Terri and Michael Schiavo were like so many other couples who meet in college, fall in love and get married. They had fun together and dreamed of starting a family. Terri worked for an insurance company and she went to church. Then one morning she collapsed on the floor of her kitchen. Paramedics arrived to find that Terri's heart had stopped, and they spent 42 minutes trying to resuscitate her, restarting her heart several times. Doctors were eventually able to stabilize her and remove the ventilator that had been used to help her breathe. At that time, they also inserted a feeding tube. Terri ended up living in this condition for 15 years.

In this video, your group will see a far different story of Terri Schiavo than what most people saw during the heart-wrenching debacle that ended with her death. Her parents' long and highly emotional struggle to save their daughter's life eventually came under the harsh glare of a worldwide media spotlight, the U.S. Congress and the Office of the President of the United States. The final outcome left everyone with difficult questions about critical ethical issues. In this video, Joni Eareckson Tada and leaders of the Joni and Friends Christian Institute on Disability respond with a biblical perspective on these life-and-death questions that affect us all.

Show the selected portions of the session 8 segment on the *Life in the Balance* DVD.

Life in the Word

Invite participants to reflect on the video. Point out that Jesus always paid close attention to the people who sought His attention. Have the group consider the Samaritan woman at the well in John 4:1-26. (If you have time, have volunteers read the passage aloud; otherwise, tell the group a summary of the story.) We can learn much about the value of knowing a person from Jesus' encounter with this woman who was an outcast. His example encourages us to always put the person first. And in the case of Terri Schiavo, she was *a person,* not merely *a case,* to be haggled over.

Discussion Question #2

Following Terri's collapse, she was unresponsive for 42 minutes. Should the paramedics have continued to try to resuscitate her? Why or why not?

Allow time for members to share their opinions. Explain to the group that this is a controversial question but one that cannot be avoided. Ask the group to try to give a biblical perspective on this point and state that the Bible teaches that all life is valuable and that the actions of the paramedics reflect that respect for life. But one of the consequences of heroic measures of this sort is the possibility of severe brain damage due to a lack of oxygen. Have the group grapple with the discussion question and then make the case that once a person has been resuscitated, we have a biblical obligation to care for that person on the basis of the value of all human life.

Discussion Question #3

What were the two primary competing interests in the Schiavo case, according to lawmakers and bioethicists?

Allow time for members to respond. Point out to the group that the two interests represent what is good versus what is right. The good is identified as the sanctity-of-life principle, and the right has to do with a competent person's entitlement to refuse medical treatment. It also involves the quality of life, to a degree. Many ethicists and families recognize the need to take into consideration the kind of life a person in a persistent coma might have. Although these families are committed to the sanctity of life, they also want to know that their loved ones are not suffering in any way.

Achieving Personal Balance

Explain to the participants that American democracy is quite a different government structure than what people were used to in biblical times. But that doesn't mean that what the Bible has to say about justice shouldn't be taken to heart; in fact, the Bible has quite a bit to say about justice. Tell the group that they should consider the role of the courts in Terri Schiavo's life and what the Bible says about justice.

Ask a volunteer to read Amos 5:24 and Micah 6:8, reminding them that righteousness, or right living, flows from God. He calls us to always act justly and mercifully.

Discussion Question #4
What is the proper role of the courts in our lives?

Allow time for members to answer. Share with the group that many argue that the courts and the government have overstepped their proper boundaries. In fact, there were at least four concerns that the general public grappled with in the complicated Schiavo case, each one of which needs to be considered from a biblical perspective:

1. The confusion and lack of medical clarity
2. The withdrawal of nutrition and hydration
3. Who should make medical decisions
4. The definition of a person

These concerns reflect a problem with knowledge, something that the Bible says is very important. The Bible teaches that true knowledge comes from the Lord, whether that is knowledge of spiritual truths, or truths about the natural realm. Proverbs (almost all of them) and Romans 1:18-32 are good texts to examine in regard to the importance of knowledge.

Discussion Question #5
Is death a natural part of life, and what should be your attitude toward death?

Allow time for members to respond. Explain to the group that the Schiavo case highlights the need to talk about what is inevitable for each of us: death. The first three chapters of Genesis reveal that death was never a part of the original creation. It is not natural. When we think of our own mortality and death, we must do so with an eye on the way we live. Read Matthew 22:37-39, and explain to the group that we must obey the two greatest commandments and let that be the measure of how we live. Being loved and loving others, especially Christ, give us a sense of fulfillment and completion. They provide us with a way of letting go of this life with anticipation for the next.

Discussion Question #6
Do you have an advance directive? Does the Bible give guidelines concerning whether or not to have an advance directive?

Allow time for members to respond. Explain that an advance directive is a document that expresses your wishes if you become sick and lose the capacity to make medical decisions.

This point echoes some of the concerns in the previous section. In a hospital setting, the problem is even more complicated. It cannot be emphasized enough how critical it is for individuals to clearly make their wishes known and to appoint someone to make medical decisions should that become necessary. Read Deuteronomy 1:13 and Acts 6:3.

Balancing Faith and Culture

Begin this next section by asking the group to discuss the following question:

Discussion Question #7

What are the goals of medicine, and why are they so important?

Allow time for group members to share their thoughts. Ideas may include heal the sick, prevent illness and disease, treat infection, improve function, alleviate pain, prevent death, and/or care for the dying.

Discussion Question #8

Should food and water be considered extraordinary or ordinary (basic) care?

Allow time for members to share their opinions. Terri Schiavo ultimately died of starvation and dehydration. She sustained a severe cognitive injury, which produced profound disability. But Terri was not terminal or suffering. These facts alone ought to give one pause to consider whether it was right to withhold nutrition and hydration from a person who was not close to death. As soon as Schiavo's case went to court, the clinical concept of "life under altered circumstances" was undermined and so was the idea of how to serve such life. Both were eclipsed by the notion of "life unworthy of life."

Discussion Question #9

Do you know anyone right now who might need someone to make medical decisions for him or her? How would you help that person?

Encourage members to share their ideas. Assure participants that according to God's Word regarding sanctity of life, every person's life is valuable to Him and to us regardless of the person's physical or mental condition. Discuss with the group the need for each of them to have an advance health care directive. Advise them that the laws governing a health care proxy are different in every state and encourage them to seek legal counsel to prepare a document that

135

states their wishes. Read John 14:1-6, and then witness to them about your personal faith in Jesus Christ, urging any participant who is not a Christian to become a Christian. Share with these individuals the hope we have as Christians to live eternally with Christ.

Discussion Question #10
How do we prepare to die?

Allow time for members to respond. Read Mark 14:33-36 and explain that while Jesus was deeply grieved over the unavoidable dying process, He submitted to the will of the Father because He knew and understood God's greater plan. The apostle Paul understood the same thing (see 2 Tim. 4:6-8). The writer of Hebrews also had this same eternal perspective and left us examples to follow (see Heb. 12).

Briefly tell about James, the brother of Jesus, who was opposed to Him as the Messiah until after His death and Resurrection. This opposition only added to the power of James's testimony later. James's life work was to win the Jews to Christ. But eventually the high priests and rulers forced James to the roof of the Temple and hurled him off the roof to his instant death.[2] Yet to this day we read the book of James for practical guidance for Christian life and conduct.

The group members need to trust in God for themselves! Have volunteers read John 3:16; 2 Corinthians 5:17 and 1 John 1:9. Then read 2 Corinthians 4:16-18, which encourages us to never lose heart:

Though outwardly we are wasting away, yet inwardly we are being renewed day by day. For our light and momentary troubles are achieving for us an eternal glory that far outweighs them all. So we fix our eyes not on what is seen, but on what is unseen. For what is seen is temporary, but what is unseen is eternal.

Now pass out paper and pens and encourage participants to write a three- or four-sentence eulogy for a friend or for themselves. Give the group about five minutes to do this. To get the group started, read aloud the following poignant excerpts from the eulogies of notable people.

Thomas Edison (1847-1931): "Through him the masses heard again, 'Let there be light.' He brought amusement, joy and romance to man, woman, and child. . . . From his laboratory we can truthfully say there came a supreme gift—a higher standard of life and living for the world."[3]

Erma Bombeck (1927-1996): "She was real and she brought us all down to earth gently, generously, and with brilliant humor. She is a twentieth-century political figure, and when the scholars gather hundreds of years from now to learn about us, they can't know it all if they don't read Erma."[4]

Helen Keller (1880-1968): "Although she was denied the light of day, Helen Keller cast more of the radiance of heaven than any person on this earth. . . . May we carry on in our troubled world, worthy of her deeds, her hope, and her faith—a faith of which the Lord spoke in His words, 'Then the eyes of the blind shall be opened, and the ears of the deaf unstopped.' "[5]

As you conclude, thank participants for their input on this sensitive topic. Encourage them to pray about sharing it with members of their family as God leads them.

Closing Prayer

Pray for families that are in situations where end-of-life decisions are being made.
   Pray for God to be glorified through people who are in persistent vegetative states.
   Pray for doctors to value the personhood of all patients.
   Pray for kind and compassionate caregivers for those in a persistent vegetative state.
   Ask God to help each participant become more and more like Jesus Christ.

Evaluating the Session

Were the session objectives met? What were the most pressing concerns that participants had about end-of-life issues? Were you successful in helping group members understand the importance of creating an advance directive? Was someone especially fearful of death, someone who might need some additional guidance and support? Are there any families facing end-of-life issues that may appreciate a visit from your pastor?

Recommended Resources

Raymond R. Mitsch and Lynn Brookside, *Grieving the Loss of Someone You Love: Daily Meditations to Help You Through the Grieving Process* (Ventura, CA: Regal, 1993).

Joni Eareckson Tada, *Heaven: Your Real Home* (Grand Rapids, MI: Zondervan, 1997).

Joni Eareckson Tada, *Heaven: Your Real Home Devotional Edition* (Grand Rapids, MI: Zondervan, 1997).

Randy Alcorn, *Heaven* (Wheaton, IL: Tyndale, 2004).

Randy Alcorn, *If God Is Good: Faith in the Midst of Suffering and Evil* (Colorado Springs, CO: Multnomah Books, 2009).

Joni Eareckson Tada, *The Life and Death Dilemma: Families Facing Health Care Choices* (Grand Rapids, MI: Zondervan, 1995).

Helpful Websites

Hospice: For patients and families facing life-threatening illness: www.hospicenet.org

Mayo Clinic Hospice Care: http://www.mayoclinic.com/health/hospice-care/HQ00860

DISCUSSION QUESTIONS

Question 1: Why do you think that stories like Karen Quinlan's, Nancy Cruzan's and Terri Schiavo's captured such national attention?

Question 2: Following Terri's collapse, she was unresponsive for 42 minutes. Should the paramedics have continued to try to resuscitate her? Why or why not?

Question 3: What were the two primary competing interests in the Schiavo case, according to lawmakers and bioethicists?

Question 4: What is the proper role for the courts in our lives?

Question 5: Is death a natural part of life, and what should be your attitude toward death?

Question 6: Do you have an advance directive? Does the Bible give guidelines concerning whether or not to have an advance directive?

Question 7: What are the goals of medicine, and why are they so important?

Question 8: Should food and water be considered extraordinary or ordinary (basic) care?

Question 9: Do you know anyone right now who might need someone to make medical decisions for him or her? How would you help that person?

Question 10: How do we prepare to die?

I'VE GOT QUESTIONS ABOUT THE AMERICAN DREAM: MATERIALISM

So do not worry, saying, "What shall we eat" or "What shall we drink?" or "What shall we wear?"
For the pagans run after all these things, and your heavenly Father knows that you need them.
But seek first his kingdom and his righteousness, and all these things will be given to you as well.

MATTHEW 6:31-33

Life-Coach Leaders

From our tenacity to our generosity, America has fascinated the rest of the world since its inception. The American dream of rising from nothing to greatness, largely by virtue of talent and hard work, is part of our distinct character. This dream has been leveraged as a powerful marketing tool to sell everything from cigarettes to prefab houses to political candidates. It resonates in advertising in ways that are so ingrained as to be barely detectable.[1] Unfortunately, the dream has gotten skewed into an attitude of entitlement and accumulation. We are inundated with messages framing happiness as a commodity. Yet

> *He is no fool who gives what he cannot keep to gain what he cannot lose.*
> JIM ELLIOT

somehow this happiness seems to remain just out of reach for many of us. A lot of people think, *Once I make this certain amount of money, then I'll be happy.* Or they believe, *When I get a bigger house, then I'll be happy.*

Scripture, however, teaches us a different perspective on contentment and joy. Pastor John Piper, in his book *Don't Waste Your Life*, describes this perspective: "God created me and you—to live with a single, all-embracing, all-transforming passion—namely, a passion to glorify God by enjoying and displaying his supreme excellence in all the spheres of life." Piper concludes that any other aim—money, fame, status, even evangelism—is futile, if we are not primarily seeking to glorify God.[2]

What Are the Session Objectives?

In this session on materialism, participants will . . .

· Learn to recognize the signs of conspicuous consumption in their lives
· Understand the steps families can take to enjoy a simple, balanced lifestyle
· Grasp how God calls each of us to be a servant of our fellow men and women

Why Should Participants Care?

·   By age 6, children can identify over 200 brand names and accumulate an average of 70 new toys a year.[3]
·   Children 8 to 13 watch an average of 40,000 commercials annually.[4]
·   The average time spent shopping per week is 6 hours, but the average time spent playing with children is only 40 minutes.[5]
·   Americans comprise 5 percent of the world's population but consume 30 percent of the world's resources.[6]
·   Only 8 percent of all humans own a car; the percentage of American households that own at least one car is 89 percent.[7]

- The world's wealthiest 20 percent consume 76.6 percent of all private consumption, while the world's poorest 20 percent consume only 1.5 percent of private consumption.[8]

Life in Real Time: Learning About Materialism

The story goes that John D. Rockefeller, considered by many to be the richest man of all time, was once asked, "How much money is enough money?" His answer: "Just a little bit more." And so it goes. Americans have had things supersized to the point where we have lost perspective. Bigger doesn't necessarily seem better, and enough never seems to be enough these days. For some people, the typical American dream has evolved in recent years to mean four bedrooms, two luxury vehicles, and a television in every room. To pay for these necessary accoutrements, both parents usually work, and children grow up spending more time with caretakers than with their parents. Our intentions were good. But what started out as a pious emphasis on hard work has faded, while getting rich has become our primary motivation.

James Truslow Adams, a Pulitzer Prize-winning historian, coined the phrase "American dream" in his 1931 book *The Epic of America*. The American dream, he wrote, is a "dream of a land in which life should be better and richer and fuller for every man, with opportunity for each according to his ability or achievement. . . . It is not a dream of motor cars and high wages merely, but a dream of a social order in which each man and each woman shall be able to attain to the fullest stature of which they are innately capable, and be recognized by others for what they are, regardless of the fortuitous circumstances of birth or position." Adams acknowledged that many had turned against this concept or distorted its purposes. His words sound prophetic since the American dream has indeed devolved into "a dream of motor cars and high wages," and numerous other excesses.[9]

Be aware that the topic of materialism can be a touchy issue and is very subjective. What some participants may see as necessity, others might see as superfluous. As the leader, your job is to guide participants in coming to realizations on their own through God's Word, discussion and the powerful illustration from the video.

Leader Checklist

- ❑ Bibles
- ❑ Copies of the statistics listed under "Why Should Participants Care?" for this session
- ❑ News headlines on economic woes, debt and/or materialism

❑ Copies of Session 9 Discussion Questions
❑ DVD keyed to session 9, "I've Got Questions"

OVERVIEW

Welcome and Opening Prayer

Welcome participants and open the session with prayer. Pray that the Holy Spirit will speak to participants about their level of materialism and consumption. Pray that they will learn to choose rightly among all their wants and embrace godly contentment with whatever the Lord provides.

Opening Activity

Hand out copies of the statistics listed under "Why Should Participants Care?" for this session. Ask the group members to tell which statistic surprised them the most and why, and which statistic surprised them the least and why. Next, hand out news headlines on economic woes, debt and/or materialism, and briefly discuss what each headline implies about the subject. Give each member a copy of the session 9 discussion questions (see page 153), and then ask the group the first discussion question.

Discussion Question #1

What is your most valuable possession?

Allow time for members to respond. Answers may include personal pictures, family heirlooms, collectibles or a wedding ring.

Share with the group that for many, the fog of consumerism and materialism has begun to lift. The economic downturn forced many people to stop and ask themselves, *What really matters? What do I need?* There is a program on the A&E television network called *Hoarders*, which takes viewers into the homes of people who have accumulated so much "stuff" that their homes are considered dangerous and unlivable. While true hoarding is rooted in psychological problems and few of us will get to that point, we need to open our eyes to our own areas of conspicuous consumption. Our homes may not be crowded with garage-sale finds or expensive antiques, but an inventory of our cluttered spaces may still expose a deep level of discontentment.

Discussion Question #2
What does "conspicuous consumption" mean?

Ask one or two members to share their ideas, and then give the following definition of conspicuous consumption: a lavish or wasteful spending thought to enhance social prestige.[10] Read Exodus 16:4 and Matthew 6:11,25-34, and then ask the third discussion question.

Discussion Question #3
What does the Bible say about our needs and consumption?

Allow time for members to respond. Point out that the Israelites were commanded to gather only enough manna for each day, and that in the Lord's Prayer we were instructed to pray for "our daily bread." Jesus also addressed our needs and our tendency to worry about them being fulfilled when He said that God will provide what we need so we don't need to worry.

Introduction to "I've Got Questions" on the *Life in the Balance* DVD

In this session's video, your group will meet a very successful young man with godly perspective, despite his extremely trying circumstances. Nick Vujicic is a businessman with a college education, an author and an international speaker, who has inspired millions of people. He travels the globe, meeting with world leaders. Nick's website gets millions of hits, and he achieved all of this before his twenty-fifth birthday. Oh, there is one other thing about Nick: He was born with no arms and no legs. Nick asked himself a lot of questions as he grew up, including: *What is my purpose? What is my significance?* He saw God's purpose and significance for others but not for himself. As Nick wrestled to understand why God allowed his disability, he played the "if only" game with God: *If only God would heal me, then I could serve Him. If only I had my arms and legs, then God would be glorified.*

Thanks to Christ's power to redeem and transform, Nick is not living a life of self-pity and complacency. Today, your group will hear him explain how he found his identity in Christ once he stopped looking at what he didn't have and started looking at what he did have. Nick's life is the antithesis to the millions of lives who search for self in material things.

Nick knows that true identity is only found in a relationship with Christ. Show the session 9 segment on the *Life in the Balance* DVD.

Life in the Word

Share the following story with the group: "It was her first brand-new bicycle and the little girl loved it as much as she'd ever loved anything. It had 'Desert Rose' written on the metal frame and pastel purple roses scattered on the white paint. She loved it even more because it was a gift from her father, not long after her parents had divorced. She took her first ride on a hot summer day, beaming with pride and joy. When she returned home, she put the kickstand down and ran inside for a quick drink. When she came back out minutes later, the bike was gone."

Discussion Question #4
Have you ever experienced a robbery or a break-in?

Allow time for members to share brief personal stories. Explain to the group that although our heart probably goes out to the little girl in the story, we shouldn't be shocked by what happened. The Bible teaches us that our treasures in this world are very easily stolen. It's obviously still a shame that it happened, and there's certainly nothing wrong with having a bike—or a home or anything else that we take great pride in. But we also need to keep the perspective that it is stuff, and stuff may get stolen or rust or be destroyed.

Read Matthew 6:19-21 and 1 Timothy 6:6-10. Point out to the group members that the real problem is not acquiring a lot of possessions but loving our possessions above all else—when we care more about our stuff than our Lord or other people. God has created all things for our enjoyment, and He blesses His children with these things. We are to enjoy His creation, but as Paul wrote, "People who want to get rich fall into temptations. . . . For the love of money is a root of all kinds of evil" (1 Tim. 6:9-10). Many people misquote this verse as saying "money is the root of all evil," but Paul emphasizes that it is the focus of the heart that determines whether or not we fall into evil. It's about where a person places his or her love.

Achieving Personal Balance

Remind the group of what they saw in the video. Ask if they noticed that Nick didn't really grasp that he was different until he started kindergarten and the other children began to tease him. He credits his mother for his undeniable confidence and knowledge that he was created by God. His anger toward God didn't dissolve, however, until he finally got past trying to negotiate with Him. As previously mentioned, Nick played, as many of us do, the "if only" game. In our version of the game, we might think, *If only God would get me out of debt, then I could* . . . Nick says he finally got to the place where he no longer prayed for God to heal him and give him arms and legs, because he was able to find purpose in his circumstances. "I think more people have a disability than they think," Nick explained. "The greatest disability that I had was not that I had no arms or legs. The greatest disability is your mindset, your choices that you make."

Help the participants understand that when we give up and stop trying, or we get discouraged when we fail, or we believe the lies that we're not good enough, then we suffer the ultimate disability.

Discussion Question #5

What's on your "if only" game board?

Allow time for members to share, and then tell the group to keep Nick's story in mind as they consider their answer to the next discussion question.

Discussion Question #6

Can you trust in God's sovereignty as Nick did? Are you prepared to trust God, even when His answer is no?

Allow time for members to answer. Explain to the group that in our instant-gratification society, we don't like to wait, and we certainly don't like to be told no. But it wasn't until Nick learned to fully trust in God's sovereignty that he was able to find his purpose. Once Nick's focus was taken off his physical disability and personal struggles, God was able to begin using him to share His message with others. "That's the great victory," says Nick, "when you can put your faith in God's grace, in God's plan, even when you don't understand."

Explain that when we discover that our lives can be hidden in Christ, the power of selfishness is broken and replaced with godly contentment (see Col. 3:3). Read Philippians 4:11-13. Discuss how we experience God's peace as we discover that we are an heir with Christ, a worshiper of God, a lover and a servant of others. In a world of consumers and materialism, we can know who we are—and to whom we belong. And, as the commercial would say, that's priceless!

Ask the group members if there's anyone willing to share an example of a time when God said no, and upon reflection that answer was obviously for his or her benefit. Before volunteers answer, give an example from your own life or the life of someone you know. Allow as many volunteers to briefly tell their story as you have time for.

Balancing Faith and Culture

Go over with the group the differences between the secular and biblical worldviews of materialism. Give the secular view and have volunteers respond with the biblical perspective.

SECULAR WORLDVIEW	BIBLICAL WORLDVIEW
More, more, more	God provides what we need
Mine, mine, mine	We are simply stewards
King of the mountain	Servant of all

Remind the group that in session 9 in the *Life in the Balance* book, Steve Bundy recalls a living example of servanthood that he witnessed as a college student at Bethany College of Missions. Many students participated in a work-study program to help with their tuition. Students were not allowed to choose their jobs; they were randomly assigned. Some of those students worked in the cafeteria collecting and washing dishes. As Steve stood in line for lunch one day, he heard loud complaints coming from a student worker who clearly didn't like his job. It was the typical whining of someone who thought he shouldn't be expected to stoop so low as to wash dishes. The student obviously had a different job in mind that was more "worthy" of his talent, and he was letting everyone know about it.

Harold Brokke, the president of the university, was also in the line at that time, and at the high point of the student's proclamation, President Brokke put down his tray, took off his suit jacket, rolled up his sleeves, and walked over to the sink next to the whining student. Then he simply took over the task of washing dishes.

Steve says he realized that serving means taking one's self out of the center of things and placing others first, and he was reminded of Jesus' example in taking the lowly position of foot washer for His disciples.

Tell the group the narrative of John 13:1-17, which starts off with Jesus at the head of the table for His last supper with His disciples. He was the most powerful person in the room, and everyone was hanging on His every word. What did He do with that powerful moment? He got up, removed His robe and washed the disciples' feet. He seized the opportunity to model being responsible with power. He looked for a way to leverage His power for the benefit of those in the room. The disciples were stunned by His humility, assuming the role of the lowliest servant.[11] Read John 13:12-17:

> When he had finished washing their feet, he put on his clothes and returned to his place. "Do you understand what I have done for you?" he asked them. "You call me 'Teacher' and 'Lord,' and rightly so, for that is what I am. Now that I, your Lord and Teacher, have washed your feet, you also should wash one another's feet. I have set you an example that you should do as I have done for you. I tell you the truth, no servant is greater than his master, nor is a messenger greater than the one who sent him. Now that you know these things, you will be blessed if you do them.

Help your group realize what God requires of each one of them as a servant. Help them to also recognize that the incredible mercy and grace of God creates a life of humility. And humility produces a servant's heart. Instead of being in bondage to our possessions, our possessions should be used to serve others.

Discussion Question #7
Why is being a humble servant so hard?

Allow time for members to respond. Tell the group that in all honesty, most of them are probably thinking, *Yes, this all makes sense. I only want to serve one master. I want to be transformed and not conformed to the world, but why is it so hard?* One reason is that when sin entered our human heart, it destroyed that pure, unadulterated identity we had of being one with our Creator (see Gen. 3). This loss of identity feeds our inner hunger—our desire to find wholeness in ourselves and even in material things. Read Matthew 19:16-24 and explain that like the rich young ruler in Matthew 19, we let our identity mesh with our "must haves."

Now read 1 John 2:15-17. Explain that our lustful desires do not come from our heavenly Father but from the secular world. The consequences that come from acting on these evil cravings are of our own making. Our fallen nature instinctively takes charge, unless we intentionally take action to be formed into the image of Christ.

Discussion Question #8
What would an honest inventory of your beliefs and your level of materialism look like on a balance sheet? How would they compare?

Give participants an opportunity for reflection, and then read Psalm 139:23-24. Tell the group that anyone consumed by materialism would do well to pray those verses every day.

Closing Prayer

As you conclude, ask participants for prayer requests they wish to share with the group.

Read Proverbs 30:8-9 aloud, and ask God to penetrate the hearts of group members. Encourage the participants to pray for one another in the week ahead as God continues to speak to them about this important topic.

Pray for those who do not have the necessities of life, much less the luxuries that many of us enjoy.

Pray that all people will seek God's wisdom to be good stewards of all that God has provided.

Evaluating the Session

Were the session objectives met? Did the discussion questions address the issues raised by participants? Did the participants seem to accept the challenges posed? Was there anyone who seemed particularly moved by the topic and might need follow-up?

Recommended Resources

Dan B. Allender, *Leading with a Limp: Turning Your Struggles into Strengths* (Colorado Springs, CO: Waterbrook Press, 2006).

John Piper, *Don't Waste Your Life* (Wheaton, IL: Crossway Books, 2003).

Dave Ramsey, *The Total Money Makeover: A Proven Plan for Financial Fitness* (Nashville, TN: Thomas Nelson, 2007).

John MacArthur, *Hard to Believe: The High Cost and Infinite Value of Following Jesus* (Nashville, TN: Thomas Nelson, 2006).

Helpful Websites

Crown Financial Ministries: www.crown.org

Financial Peace University: http://www.daveramsey.com/fpu

DISCUSSION QUESTIONS

Question 1:   What is your most valuable possession?

Question 2:   What does "conspicuous consumption" mean?

Question 3:   What does the Bible say about our needs and consumption?

Question 4:   Have you ever experienced a robbery or break-in?

Question 5:   What's on your "if only" game board?

Question 6:   Can you trust in God's sovereignty as Nick did? Are you prepared to trust God, even when His answer is no?

Question 7:   Why is being a humble servant so hard?

Question 8:   What would an honest inventory of your beliefs and your level of materialism look like on a balance sheet? How would they compare?

NOW WHAT?

He has showed you, O Man, what is good,
And what does the Lord require of you?
To act justly and to love mercy and to walk humbly with your God.

MICAH 6:8

Life-Coach Leaders

After leading your small group through each session and completing the evaluation, you're ready to encourage the group to put their faith into action. But a watching world, which once applauded people of faith as heroes, now looks on with skepticism. A conservative stand on the issues we've discussed may not be popular. So let us draw our eyes upward to where there is a great crowd of witnesses who have gone on before us and are now surrounding us, and let's also keep our eyes on Jesus, who alone can make our steps of faith perfectly fulfill His plan (see Heb. 12:1-2).

Everyone wants to be a hero, don't they? We assume they do, but if that's true, then why is it commonly understood that 20 percent of the people do the work of the ministry while 80 percent simply warm a church pew? If you can help just one participant take a new step of faith and make a decision to serve a person he or she may have walked past before this study, you can rejoice. Jesus was not able to motivate everyone He met to move beyond apathy. But those who followed Him were forever changed because they caught a vision of God's plan for a fallen world. They stood at a crossroad and chose life!

What Are the Session Objectives?

In this session on Christian advocacy, participants will . . .

- Examine specific ideas of what God wants this world to look like
- Take steps to show God's justice, mercy and righteousness in practical ways
- Determine to safeguard the life and dignity of every human being
- Understand Christian advocacy and unite with others for truth and change

Why Should Participants Care?

"Our Father in heaven, hallowed be your name, *your kingdom come, your will be done on earth as it is in heaven*" (Matt. 6:9-10, emphasis added). Every time participants pray the Lord's Prayer, they're asking God to make the kingdom of Christ visible on earth. They're asking, "Lord, may Your kingdom of righteousness, justice and peace come and may Your will be done here on earth exactly as You envision it in heaven . . . and give me the privilege of helping to make it happen!" It's what vision is all about—not only seeing the world as God pictures it, but also helping to bring that picture into focus and to make it *real*. As Christians, we are to be ambassadors for the kingdom of Christ. We can help make His kingdom *real* in a world currently occupied by the enemy, reclaiming earth as the King's. Each participant's goal should be to *proclaim* the gospel message as well as *portray* it. In a world of injustice, pain and poverty, each Christian is to reflect God's justice, mercy and love.

Life in Real Time: Christian Service and Advocacy

God has a mission statement for every Christian. He gifted them with abilities and talents that are to be used for the building up of the Body of Christ—the Church. Joni says this about being Christ's ambassadors:

Although Satan enslaved the citizens of earth, . . . you and I have the high privilege of freeing captive subjects and retaking earth under the Family banner. You and I are to repossess this planet under the rightful Ruler. . . . every time we advance the Gospel, we are "taking back" territory—not to mention people—that the enemy assumed were his.

There are four parts to helping participants put what they believe in action:

Conviction	Value	Ownership	Action

- Conviction is the belief that something should be done by someone. Conviction says, "It's a great idea and something we should definitely put on a future agenda for discussion and exploration."
- Value recognizes that something is important to success. Value says, "We can see how that would help us accomplish our mission."
- Ownership happens when permission is given to move forward. Ownership says, "Yes, that sounds like something Nancy could do. Let's ask her."
- Action begins when the program begins to take shape. Action says, "I will do it! Here's the plan!"[1]

Christian service can get stalled on any one of these levels, but being aware of these steps can help an individual or a church accomplish whatever goals have been set.

Leader Checklist

- ❑ Bibles
- ❑ A variety of types of eyeglasses (small, large, different magnifications, and so forth.)
- ❑ News headlines used in the previous sessions
- ❑ Session 10 discussion questions
- ❑ DVD keyed to session 10, "Now What?"
- ❑ Copies of "An Advocate's Staircase" (see page 163)

OVERVIEW

Welcome and Introductions

Welcome participants to this last session in your study. Before you begin, lead them in the prayer that our Lord taught His followers to pray: The Lord's Prayer.

Opening Activity

Have group members experiment with the various types of glasses you show them, including a few that you've smeared with dirt. Point out how this study has opened their eyes to the needs of those who suffer pain and injustice. Demonstrate how a clean pair of glasses is easier to see through than a pair of dirty ones. Finally, show participants a pair of glasses with a high degree of magnification, and point out how they sharpen our vision even more to the things that we could easily miss.

Explain to the group that prior to the study, their vision was probably limited or impaired because they were unaware of societal changes, technical advances, and the ramifications of decisions. After studying *Life in the Balance,* they will see more clearly and have an expanded view of God's plan for the unborn, victims of violence, and people with disabilities. Their eyes have been opened to their own materialistic desires, flawed self-image, and the influences that shape each of us. Pass out the news headlines used in the previous sessions, give each member a copy of the session 10 discussion questions (see page 167), and then ask the group the first discussion question.

Discussion Question #1
Which topic in this study has sharpened your focus the most?

Allow time for group members to look over the headlines and respond.

Introduction to "Now What?" on the *Life in the Balance* DVD

Briefly describe to the group what the video segment is about: Joni Eareckson Tada has some inspiring closing thoughts for the group as they consider what Christian advocacy means to each of them personally and how they might discover what God is asking them to do in the days ahead. Joni urges everyone to engage in the battle of helping people replace their heart of stone with a heart of flesh. The way people can do this is by shaking gospel salt and shining gospel light everywhere they go. One person at a time, the Church and the world can be changed for Christ. Show the session 10 segment on the *Life in the Balance* DVD.

Life in the Word

Explain that during this study, the group has attentively listened, examined the Scriptures and discussed the issues. Now the challenge is to figure out what they will do with all that they've learned. Our wonderful God is doing everything from His end to right what is wrong, but He needs us to catch His vision.

Discussion Question #2
What do you think God wants His world to look like?

Allow time for members to respond, and then lead members in exploring the following verses that show how God envisions His world:

· **Psalm 82:3-4**: A person's life and dignity are safeguarded.
· **Proverbs 14:34**: His righteousness is exalted.
· **Micah 6:8**: Justice and mercy reign.
· **Hebrews 12:14**: People live in peace.

Discussion Question #3
Our goal as Christ's ambassadors is to proclaim the gospel message throughout the world. How are we doing?

Allow several participants to share their opinions, and then read James 1:22. Encourage participants to share their various areas of ministry.

Explain to the group that their passion may not be one of the eight topics they've studied during this course. They may have a heart for people with addictions, or they may feel

> *Giving Christ to others is always a picture of Christianity with its sleeves rolled up!*
> JONI EARECKSON TADA

drawn to help homeless families. They may be especially interested in the plight of seniors, or their interests may lie in working against human trafficking or child abuse. They may feel led to help alleviate poverty or reverse the trend of illiteracy. Read Psalm 10:17, and explain that the fact that they are feeling *led* to make a difference shows that they've tapped deep into God's heart of compassion.

Discussion Question #4

How will this study change your thoughts and actions? Your conversations with neighbors and friends? How will it influence your prayer and worship?

Allow time for members to share their thoughts.

Achieving Personal Balance

Explain to the group that as members of Christ's Body, we are His visible and present hands on earth. God uses our hands, time, treasure and talents to do His work in the world.

Discussion Question #5

What is Christian advocacy?

Allow time for members to respond, and then explain that our Christian advocacy and service is part of our Christian witness. When it comes to proclaiming and portraying the gospel, advocacy can be considered part of *proclaiming* the gospel (declaring the good news), and service is *portraying* the gospel (demonstrating the good news). We cannot only preach the gospel; people must experience it. And rubber-meets-the-road Christianity involves being an advocate. If a person wanted to become an advocate in the stem cell debate, for example, here are some things he or she could do:

1. Learn more about adult stem cell research and share your views with others.
2. Contact editors and TV producers who present slanted or inaccurate views about stem cell research and share your concerns.
3. Create a watchdog task force to explore legislative bills and initiatives seeking to expand funding for embryonic stem cell research.

4. Coordinate local letter-writing parties that include people with disabilities and the elderly. Personal letters sent to district offices of state or U.S. representatives work best.

5. Connect with groups like Not Dead Yet or ADAPT to understand policies or laws that encroach on the welfare of people with disabilities and the elderly.

6. Assist people with disabilities and the elderly in writing and submitting opinion pieces and letters to newspaper editors in their state capitol and in Washington, DC.

Discussion Question #6
How can you know what God wants you to do to advocate for the weakest and most vulnerable in our society?

Allow time for group members to respond. Ideas should include identifying their personal interests and talents as well as spending time in prayer.

Read Colossians 4:4-6 and Timothy 4:12. Tell the group members to always remember that they are speaking on behalf of Jesus Christ. What good is it if we win the battle but lose people's souls in the process? Graciousness and gentleness of speech always win the day. (To reinforce this point, ahead of time enlist a member of the group to become outraged over an issue. Have the volunteer rant and rave; use name-calling; and put down groups, the media and others in a dramatic, offensive way. Once he or she has gained the attention—and negative stares—of the rest of the group, say, "Stop! We have just witnessed an example of the kind of advocacy Christians should *not* engage in!")

Explain that the art of advocacy is relationship building. Nothing is more rewarding than to witness an individual or family rise above their circumstances to find hope in Christ. The group members could perhaps facilitate a support group for them in their church. Once empowered, those individuals and families may well be the best spokespeople for effecting change in peoples' hearts and transformation in a community.

Balancing Faith and Culture

Begin this next section by asking the group to discuss the following question.

Discussion Question #7
What did Joni mean when she said that if you feel unskilled to be a spokesperson on an issue, you're just the person God is looking for?

Allow time for members to respond, and then read 1 Corinthians 1:26-29. Explain to the group that God used the weaknesses of many of the heroes of the faith to show His strength.

Through weakness, God will bring maximum glory to Himself. Heroes of the faith not only present the message of salvation, but they also help people experience salvation. Point out to the group members that they have met some of these heroes in this study. They are ordinary, everyday people who are not merely caught up in a cause—they are captivated by Christ. And they are making Him real in our world, just like Mark Trombino is doing.

Mark Trombino is outgoing, articulate and smart. He is an actor, businessman, author and also a motivational speaker. People notice Mark's dark hair and warm smile, but these things don't open doors to corporate boardrooms or college auditoriums. However, the fact that Mark is three feet three inches tall does! He has a vision to make a positive difference in the world. Mark started Motivational Small Talk to provide quality programs that focus on diversity education, preventing bullying and learning to overcome life's obstacles.

Mark knows a little something about overcoming obstacles. In 2004, his beautiful wife, Anu, was involved in a head-on automobile accident and was paralyzed from the neck down. After five months in the hospital, she died, leaving Mark to raise their one-year-old daughter. Through it all he's learned to trust in God's love and plan for his life. Today, Mark is happily remarried, and he published his first book to encourage everyone to "seize the day," which was Anu's motto. (Participants who are interested in learning more about Mark can visit his website at www.motivationalsmalltalk.com.)

Discussion Question #8

Our world needs a change of heart, a moral center and a godly vision.
How will you make Christ real in your community?

Allow time for members to share. Some members may express doubts about their abilities to truly make a difference in their world. Ask a volunteer to read Deuteronomy 30:11-14. Help members appreciate the confidence that God has in them and that, because He has placed His Word in them, they can obey it.

Point out to the group that changing hearts is the job of the Church. Culture is a reflection of what we worship, and if we want to change our culture, we must introduce people to the one and only true God who deserves our worship.

(If you have time, consider inviting the volunteer and/or mission coordinator from your church to share a few of the service opportunities available in your community. If participants show interest, discuss service projects that your group might adopt. Schedule future meetings to plan and carry out a project.)

> *This command I [God] am giving you today*
> *is not too difficult for you to understand or perform.*
> *The message is very close at hand; it is on*
> *your lips and in your heart so that you can obey it.*
> DEUTERONOMY 30:11,14, *NLT*

Closing Prayer

Thank the participants for joining you in this important study, and encourage them to continue to seek God's guidance in all of these issues.

Pass out copies of "An Advocate's Staircase" found on the next page. Explain to the group that regarding other areas of interest, they can contact groups such as National Right to Life, National Down Syndrome Congress or the Center for Bioethics and Human Dignity. Tell the participants that from such organizations, they will be able to find out what policies are encroaching on the welfare of people who can't speak for themselves. Suggest that group members also do an Internet search for contact information for organizations that interest them.

Because this session was a time for participants to examine their heart for service, make the closing prayer time especially meaningful to your group. Be sure to plan enough time for people to express their personal prayer requests.

- Pray against the temptation to despair when moving among people in the grip of weakness and injustice.
- Ask God to cultivate a love for hurting people throughout your church and community.
- Ask God to keep the participants from a spirit of bitterness toward perpetrators of abusive situations.
- Praise God for the weaknesses we have that cause us to draw closer to Him and depend on His power in our life.
- Praise God for Christian servants who advocate and stand up for justice at every level of our society and throughout the world.
- Ask God for an enlarged heart of compassion and the courage to hold up those who are weak.

An Advocate's Staircase

Here are some practical steps to becoming an advocate. Begin at the bottom.

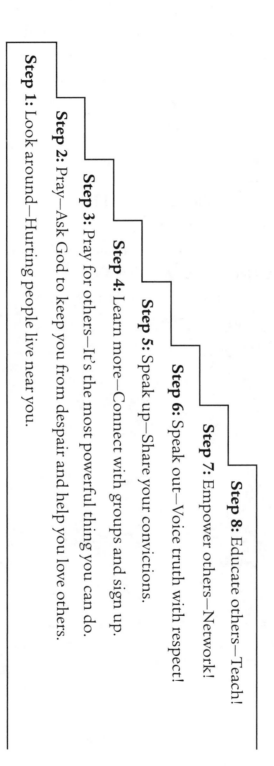

Step 8: Educate others—Teach!

Step 7: Empower others—Network!

Step 6: Speak out—Voice truth with respect!

Step 5: Speak up—Share your convictions.

Step 4: Learn more—Connect with groups and sign up.

Step 3: Pray for others—It's the most powerful thing you can do.

Step 2: Pray—Ask God to keep you from despair and help you love others.

Step 1: Look around—Hurting people live near you.

For other areas of interest, contact groups such as the National Right to Life (www.nrlc.org), National Down Syndrome Congress (www.ndsccenter.org), or the Center for Bioethics and Human Dignity (www.cbhd.org).

Evaluating the Session

Were participants able to describe God's vision for our world? Did the group members see their weaknesses as part of God's plan? Could you identify changes in the hearts of participants through this study? Were they acknowledged and celebrated? Will this session help participants share their faith with others?

Helpful Websites

Advocacy, Inc.: www.advocacyinc.org

Center for Bioethics and Human Dignity: www.cbhd.org

Child Advocates: www.childadvocates.org

Motivational Small Talk Inc.: www.motivationalsmalltalk.com

National Disability Rights Network: www.ndrn.org

National Down Syndrome Congress: www.ndsccenter.org

National Right to Life: www.nrlc.org

World Vision: www.worldvision.org

SESSION 10

DISCUSSION QUESTIONS

Question 1: Which topic in this study has sharpened your focus the most?

Question 2: What do you think God wants His world to look like?

Question 3: Our goal as Christ's ambassadors is to proclaim the gospel message throughout the world. How are we doing?

Question 4: How will this study change your thoughts and actions? Your conversations with neighbors and friends? How will it influence your prayer and worship?

Question 5: What is Christian advocacy?

Question 6: How can you know what God wants you to do to advocate for the weakest and most vulnerable in our society?

Question 7: What did Joni mean when she said that if you feel unskilled to be a spokesperson on an issue, you're just the person God is looking for?

Question 8: Our world needs a change of heart, a moral center and a godly vision. How will you make Christ real in your community?

GLOSSARY OF TERMINOLOGY

The following are some brief definitions of terms regarding disabilities and bioethics.

advance directive: instructions given by an individual specifying what actions should be taken for his or her health in the event that the individual is no longer able to make decisions due to illness or incapacity.

Alzheimer's disease: a progressive neurological disease of the brain that leads to irreversible loss of neurons and dementia. Clinical hallmarks are progressive memory impairment, judgment, decision-making, orientation to surroundings and language. Diagnosis made on the basis of a neurologic examination, but a definitive diagnosis can only be made at autopsy.

Asperger's syndrome: an autistic disorder most notable for a discrepancy between intellectual and social abilities. Typical features may include uncoordinated motor movements, social impairment with extreme egocentricity, limited interests, topical preoccupations and expertise, repetitive routines or rituals, speech and language peculiarities and nonverbal communication problems. Sometimes referred to as high-functioning autism.

autism: a complex developmental disability that typically appears during the first three years of life and is the result of a neurological disorder that affects the normal functioning of the brain, impacting development in the areas of social interaction, communication skills and sensory integration. Both children and adults with autism typically show difficulties in verbal and nonverbal communication, social interactions, and leisure or play activities.

autism spectrum disorders: a range of neurological disorders that most markedly involve some degree of difficulty with communication and interpersonal relationships, as well as obsessions and repetitive behaviors. Individuals range from lower to higher functioning. Diagnoses include autism, Asperger's syndrome, Rett syndrome, childhood disintegrative disorder and pervasive developmental disorder.

behavior modification: usually a one-on-one intensive, structured teaching program for children with autism spectrum disorder or other disabilities, using reinforced practice of different skills. Can be called applied behavior analysis, discrete trial therapy, functional communication training, incidental teaching, behavior chaining or errorless learning, among others.

bioethicist: a person who studies the ethical and moral implications of new biological discoveries and biomedical advances.

cerebral palsy: a term used to describe a group of chronic conditions affecting body movements and muscle coordination. It is caused by damage to one or more specific areas of the brain, usually occurring during fetal development or infancy. It can also occur before, during or shortly following birth.

developmental disabilities: severe, chronic disabilities attributed to mental or physical impairments (or a combination of the two) occurring before adulthood and resulting in substantial functional limitations in major life activities. Examples include autism, cerebral palsy, Down syndrome, mental retardation and spina bifida.

Down syndrome: also called trisomy 21, is caused by the presence of all or part of an extra twenty-first chromosome. It is characterized by a combination of major and minor differences in structure, a particular set of facial characteristics, and is often associated with some impairment of cognitive ability, ranging from mild to severe developmental disabilities.

eugenics: the study of or belief in the possibility of improving the qualities of the human species or a human population, especially by such means as discouraging reproduction by persons having genetic defects or presumed to have inheritable undesirable traits (negative eugenics) or encouraging reproduction by persons presumed to have inheritable desirable traits (positive eugenics).

euthanasia: the act of putting to death, or allowing to die, a person with an incurable or painful disease or condition by withholding extreme medical measures or by administering a lethal dose of medication.

genocide: the deliberate and systematic extermination of a national, racial, political, religious or cultural group.

germline: the sequence of cells that develop into eggs and sperm. Also, inherited material that comes from the eggs or sperm and is passed on to offspring.

health care proxy: designation of a surrogate medical decision-maker in the event that a person becomes unable to make medical decisions on his or her own behalf.

juvenile arthritis: rheumatoid arthritis is the most common type of arthritis in children under the age of 16 and causes persistent joint pain, swelling and stiffness. Symptoms can appear for a few months or for a lifetime. Some types of juvenile rheumatoid arthritis can cause serious complications, such as growth problems and eye inflammation. Treatment focuses on controlling pain, improving function and preventing joint damage.

Manhattan Declaration: a 4,700-word declaration speaking in defense of the sanctity of life, traditional marriage and religious liberty, released on November 20, 2009, by a group of prominent Christian clergy, ministry leaders and scholars. It issues a call to Christians to adhere firmly to their convictions in these areas. (See pages 19-22 for a summary, or read the entire document at http://manhattandeclaration.org/read. aspx.)

materialism: a preoccupation with or emphasis on material objects, comforts and considerations, with a disinterest in or rejection of spiritual, intellectual or cultural values.

multiple sclerosis (MS): a disease of the central nervous system marked by numbness, weakness, loss of muscle coordination and problems with vision, speech and bladder control. MS is an autoimmune disease in which the body's immune system attacks myelin, a key substance that serves as a nerve insulator and helps in the transmission of nerve signals. The progress, severity and specific symptoms in MS are unpredictable. One never knows when attacks will occur, how long they will last or how severe they will be.

muscular dystrophy (MD): a term used to describe a number of inherited disorders characterized by progressive weakness and wasting of the muscles. The most common and severe type is Duchenne's MD, in which a genetic defect leads to the formation of an abnormal type of muscle protein called dystrophin and is progressive and terminal.

Parkinson's disease: a slowly progressive neurologic disease characterized by a fixed, inexpressive face; tremor while resting; slowing of voluntary movements; a gait with short, accelerating steps; peculiar posture and muscle weakness—all caused by a degeneration of an area of the brain called the basal ganglia and by low production of the neurotransmitter dopamine.

pervasive developmental disorder (PDD): a category of neurological disorders characterized by severe and pervasive impairment in several areas of development and included as an autism spectrum disorder.

picture exchange communication system (PECs): a form of augmentative and alternate communication that uses pictures instead of words to help children communicate. PECs was designed especially for children with autism who have delays in speech development.

pre-implantation genetic diagnosis (PGD): a procedure used in conjunction with in vitro fertilization to screen for specific genetic or chromosomal abnormalities, or gender, before transferring the fertilized eggs into the mother.

quadriplegic: a person who is paralyzed and has partial or total loss of use of legs, arms and torso, with both sensation and control of movement being affected.

Rett syndrome: an inherited developmental disorder, usually observed only in females, that is characterized by a short period of normal development, followed by loss of developmental skills (particularly purposeful hand movements) and marked psychomotor retardation. A brief autistic-like phase may be observed during the preschool period, but the subsequent course and clinical features are markedly different from autism, although it is included as an autism spectrum disorder.

ritualistic behaviors: restricted, repetitive and stereotyped behaviors that present themselves as obsessive interests, rigid adherence to routines, stereotyped motor movements and preoccupation with parts of or whole objects.

sensory integration: a neurological process that organizes sensation from one's own body and the environment, making it possible to make sense of the environment. Children with autism have trouble learning to do this, with some senses being excessively hypersensitive and others hyposensitive. Sensory integration therapy is a form of occupational therapy that is specifically designed to stimulate and challenge all of the senses to work together.

social scripts: also known as social stories, an intervention strategy to help teach children with autism spectrum disorder self-awareness, self-calming and self-management skills. Usually written with the child, they target social situations that are difficult for the child to navigate and tell a story from beginning to end with a desired outcome. Creating, reading and practicing a social script can help a child learn how to achieve that desired outcome.

spectrum disorder: a group of disorders with similar features and causation, ranging from mild to severe symptoms.

spina bifida: a congenital (present at birth) malformation in which there is a bony defect in the vertebral column so that part of the spinal cord is exposed. People with spina bifida can have bladder and bowel incontinence, cognitive and learning problems and limited mobility.

stem cell: a cell that, upon division, replaces its own numbers and also gives rise to cells that differentiate further into one or more specialized types—a master, or blank slate, cell that is very pliable and has the ability to change into almost any other kind of body tissue. Stem cells can be retrieved from adult tissues or human embryos.

utilitarianism: the doctrine that virtue is based on utility and that conduct should be directed toward promoting the greatest good and happiness for the greatest number of persons, while sacrificing the weak and vulnerable in order to do so.

Zellweger syndrome: an inherited condition that damages the white matter of the brain and also affects how the body metabolizes particular substances in the blood and organ tissues, causing neurological abnormalities, facial deformities and lack of muscle tone among other problems. There is no cure and no treatment. Most will die by six months of age.

ENDNOTES

Getting Started

1. "Issues: People Living with Disabilities," A message from Joni Eareckson Tada, The Lausaane Movement. http://www.lausanne.org/issue-people-with-disabilities/overview.html.
2. "Pregnancy and Newborn Health Education Center: Birth Defects," The March of Dimes. http://www.marchofdimes.com/pnhec/4439_1206.asp.
3. "What Is Autism? Facts and Stats," Autism Society, 2003. http://www.education.com/reference/article/Ref_What_Autism_Facts/.
4. "War on Terror," Wikipedia. http://en.wikipedia.org/wiki/War_on_Terror.
5. Mark W. Baker, Ph.D., "Dealing with the Emotions of Those with Special Needs," Beyond Suffering: Christian View on Disability Ministry, by Joni and Friends Christian Institute on Disability, 2010.

The Manhattan Declaration: A Summary

1. Copyright © 2010 Manhattan Declaration. All rights reserved. Used with permission. http://www.ManhattanDeclaration.org.

Session 2: When Life Isn't Fair: Violence in the Streets

1. "2009 Statistics," Rape Abuse and Incest National Network, 2009. http://www.rainn.org/statistics (accessed May 14, 2010).
2. "2009 Statistics," Gang Facts and Statistics. http://www.helpinggangyouth.com/statistics.html (accessed May 14, 2010).
3. "National Child Abuse Statistics," Childhelp. http://www.childhelp.org/resources/learning-center/statistics (accessed May 14, 2010).
4. Matthew R. Durose et al., "Family Violence Statistics: Including Statistics on Strangers and Acquaintances," Bureau of Justice Statistics, June 12, 2005. http://bjs.ojp.usdoj.gov/index.cfm?ty=pbdetail&iid=828 (accessed May 14, 2010).
5. Richard J. Bonnie and Robert B. Wallace, eds., *Elder Mistreatment: Abuse, Neglect and Exploitation in an Aging America,* Committee on National Statistics and Behavioral and Social Sciences and Education, 2003.
6. "School Crime Victimization," Office of Juvenile Justice and Delinquency Prevention, October 31, 2009. http://ojjdp.ncjrs.gov/ojstatbb/victims/qa02201.asp?qaDate=2006 (accessed May 14, 2010).
7. D. Sobsey et al, *Violence and Disability: An Annotated Bibliography* (Baltimore, MD: Brookes Publishing, 1995).
8. David Powlison, *Anger: Escaping the Maze,* Resources for Changing Lives, The Christian Counseling Education Foundation (Phillipsburg, NJ: P&R Publishing, 2000), p. 3.

Session 3: Making Sense of Autism

1. Sarah Stup, *Are Your Eyes Listening?* (Frederick, MD: SarahStup.com, 2007), quoted in Aaron Notarianni Stephens, "Silent Echoes," *Exceptional Parents,* vol. 38, no. 10, October 2008, p. 25.
2. "Barbara Newman Interview," *Making Sense of Autism, Part 2* (Joni and Friends DVDTV30).
3. Sarah Stup, *Are Your Eyes Listening?* (Frederick, MD: SarahStup.com, 2007), quoted in Aaron Notarianni Stephens, "Silent Echoes," *Exceptional Parents,* vol. 38, no. 10, October 2008, p. 25.
4. "Barbara Newman Interview," *Making Sense of Autism, Part 2* (Joni and Friends DVDTV30).

Session 4: Self-Image in a Fickle Culture

1. Jessica Bennett and Cara Phillips, "Unattainable Beauty: The Decade's Most Egregious Retouching Scandal," *Newsweek,* 2010. http://www.newsweek.com/id/231629 (accessed May 24, 2010). (Note: The images that accompany this article may not be appropriate for all audiences.) For more information about the Dove Campaign for Real Beauty, visit www.campaignforrealbeauty.com.
2. C. S. Lewis, *The Screwtape Letters* (San Francisco, CA: HarperCollins, 2001), p. 107.
3. Ralph C. Wood, "The Triumph of the Eye," *Christian Reflection: A Series in Faith and Ethics* (Waco, TX: The Center for Christian Ethics at Baylor University, 2009).
4. *Merriam-Webster Online Dictionary,* 2010, s.v. "self-image." http://www.merriam-webster.com/dictionary/self-image.
5. Copyright © 2010 Manhattan Declaration. All rights reserved. Used with permission. http://www.ManhattanDeclaration.org.

Session 5: Searching for the Greater Good: The Stem Cell Debate

1. Levin, Yuval, "Public Opinion and the Embryo Debates," *The New Atlantis: A Journal of Technology & Society.* http://www.thenewatlantis.com/publications/public-opinion-and-the-embryo-debates.
2. Joni and Friends Christian Institute on Disability, "Position on Embryonic Stem Cell Research," *Joni and Friends International Disability Center,* March 10, 2009. http://www.joniandfriends.org/09_REVISED-ESC.pdf.
3. *Lives in the Balance: The Stem Cell Debate* (Joni and Friends DVDTV22)

Session 6: The Truth Behind the Pain of Abortion

1. CDC information for 2004 statistics drawn from special supplement "Abortion Surveillance—United States, 2004," *Morbidity and Mortality Weekly Report,* vol. 56, no. SS09 (November 23, 2007) and earlier reports, quoted in *Abortion Statistics: United States Data and Trends.* http://www.nrlc.org/Factsheets/FS03_AbortionInTheUS.pdf (accessed May 15, 2010).
2. Jessica Lawlor, "Long-Term Physiological and Psychological Effects of Abortion on Women," Central Illinois Right to Life. http://www.cirtl.org/syndrome.htm (accessed May 15, 2010).

Session 7: A Calloused Conscience: Eugenics and Genocide

1. This poem, attributed to Pastor Martin Niemöller, is about the Nazi regime's purging of group after group, while the German intellectuals did nothing.
2. Susan W. Enouen, "Down Syndrome and Abortion," PhysiciansForLife.org, 2004-2010. http://www.physiciansforlife.org/content/view/1301/26/ (accessed May 15, 2010).
3. "Convention on the Prevention and Punishment of the Crimes of Genocide," Wikipedia, May 8, 2010. http://en.wikipedia.org/wiki/Convention_on_ the_Prevention_and_Punishment_of_the_Crime_of_Genocide (accessed May 15, 2010). Italics added for emphasis.
4. Children's Holocaust Memorial & Paper Clip Project at Whitwell Middle School, "The Beginning," 2010. http://69.8.250.59/homepage _pc.cfm?id=78 (accessed May 15, 2010).
5. "Paper Clip Project," Wikipedia. http://en.wikipedia.org/wiki/Paper_Clips_Project (accessed May 15, 2010).
6. United States Holocaust Memorial Museum, "Handicapped" (Washington, DC: United States Holocaust Memorial Museum, 2009), brochure.
7. Hugh Gregory Gallagher, *By Trust Betrayed: Patients, Physicians, and the License to Kill in the Third Reich,* rev. ed. (St. Petersburg, FL: Vandamere Press, 1995).
8. Dan Allender, *Leading with a Limp* (Colorado Springs, CO: WaterBrook Press, 2006), pp. 46,48.
9. See http://www.youtube.com/watch?v=l6Zh7xlc0ho.

Session 8: From Obscurity to Celebrity by Way of Tragedy: End-of-Life Issues

1. Wikipedia, s.v. "hospice." http://en.wikipedia.org/wiki/Hospice.
2. Henrietta C. Mears, *What the Bible Is All About* (Ventura, CA: Regal Books, 1983), p. 574.
3. Cyrus M. Copeland, ed. *Farewell, Godspeed: The Greatest Eulogies of Our Time* (New York: Harmony Books 2003), p. 173.
4. Ibid., p. 258.
5. Ibid., p. 48.

Session 9: I've Got Questions About the American Dream: Materialism

1. Larry Kaagan and Patricia Graham, "Chasing the American Dream," *Know* magazine, vol. 1, no. 2, (Fall/Winter 2004). http://www.knowledgenet works.com/know/2004/fall/article8.html.
2. John Piper, *Don't Waste Your Life* (Wheaton, IL: Crossway Books, 2003), p. 31.
3. Juliet Schor, *Born to Buy: The Commercialized Child and the New Consumer Culture* (New York: Simon and Schuster, 2004), p. 19, quoted in Crown Financial Services, "Materialism vs. Self Esteem," Crown Financial Services, 2010. http://www.crown.org/library (accessed May 15, 2010).
4. Ibid.
5. Betsy Morris, "Big Spenders: As a Favored Pastime, Shopping Ranks High with Most Americans," *Wall Street Journal,* July 30, 1987, quoted in "All-Consuming Passion: Waking Up from the American Dream," *EcoFuture,* January 7, 2002. http://www.ecofuture.org/pk/pkar9506.html#acp-foot (accessed May 15, 2010).
6. Denis Hayes, "Economic Power," *Seattle Weekly,* November 10, 1993, p. 15, quoted in "All-Consuming Passion: Waking Up from the American Dream," *EcoFuture,* January 7, 2002. http://www.ecofuture.org/pk/pkar9506.html#acp-foot (accessed May 15, 2010). Alan Durning, "Asking How Much Is Enough," in Lester R. Brown et al, *State of the World 1991* (New York: W.W. Norton and Co. Inc., 2001), p. 158, quoted in "All-Consuming Passion: Waking Up from the American Dream," *EcoFuture,* January 7, 2002. http://www.ecofuture.org/pk/pkar9506.html#acp-foot (accessed May 15, 2010).
7. Jeremy Rifkin, ed., *The Green Lifestyle Handbook* (New York: Henry Hold and Company, 1990), p. 33, quoted in "All-Consuming Passion: Waking Up from the American Dream," *EcoFuture,* January 7, 2002. http://www.ecofuture.org/pk/pkar9506.html#acp-foot (accessed May 15, 2010).
8. Anup Shah, "Consumption and Consumerism," *Global Issues,* September 3, 2008. http://www.globalissues.org/issue/235/consumption-and-consumerism (accessed May 15, 2010).
9. Richard O'Mara, "The Evolution of the American Dream," *The Christian Science Monitor,* September 29, 2008. http://www.csmonitor.com/Commentary/Opinion/2008/0929/p09s03-coop.html (accessed May 15, 2010).
10. *Merriam-Webster Online,* 2010, s.v. "conspicuous consumption." http://www.merriam-webster.com/netdict/conspicuous%20consumption.
11. "The Most Powerful Man in the Room" Message from Andy Stanley, Catalyst Conference, 2007. See http://www.youtube.com/watch?v=0fu106PcwQM.

Session 10: Now What?

1. Jim Pierson, et al., *Special Needs, Special Ministry: For Children's Ministry* (Loveland, CO: Group Publishing, 2004), pp. 34-35. Originally developed by Dr. Scott Daniels and Dr. Steve Green.

ABOUT JONI AND FRIENDS
INTERNATIONAL DISABILITY CENTER

Joni Eareckson Tada is the founder of the Joni and Friends International Disability Ministry and an advocate for the disability community that numbers 660 million people worldwide.

Our Mission

The mission of the Joni and Friends International Disability Center is to communicate the gospel and equip Christ-honoring churches worldwide to evangelize and disciple people affected by disabilities:

- We present the clear and concise gospel of Jesus Christ to all people with disabilities and their families served through our programs.
- We train, disciple and mentor people affected by disability to exercise their gifts of leadership and service in the Church and their communities.
- We energize the Church to move from lack of awareness to including persons with disabilities into the fabric of worship, fellowship and outreach.

The Christian Institute on Disability

Leaders in the Church and community have long looked to Joni Eareckson Tada and Joni and Friends as an authoritative Christian voice on critical issues of disability. To carry the work of education and advocacy to the next level, the Joni and Friends International Disability Center has established the Christian Institute on Disability to aggressively promote a Christ-centered, biblical approach that protects human dignity and the sanctity of all human life, no matter what the disabling condition.

The mission of the Christian Institute on Disability is to impact the Church, Christian and public institutions and societies with a biblical worldview and life-giving truth on issues pertaining to life, dignity, justice and equality that affect people with disabilities. This mission is carried out through education programs in churches, colleges and seminaries.

Beyond Suffering: Christian Views on Disability Ministry

The 32-hour Certificate in Disability Ministry, awarded by the Christian Institute on Disability, is designed to give participants an introductory understanding of the aspects of disabilities. *Beyond Suffering* is comprised of four thought-provoking modules: Overview of Disability, Theology of Disability, Church and Disability, and Introduction to Bioethics. Participants will learn through lecture, group discussion, video and hands-on experience how to evangelize and empower those affected by disability. This program is designed for ministers, professionals, teachers, volunteers, students and anyone interested in learning more about effective disability ministry.

Joni and Friends International Disability Center
PO Box 3333
Agoura Hills, California 91376-3333
www.joniandfriends.org

818-707-5664